James Pennebaker's long-awaited Writing to Heal *is a treasure, the single most important on my shelf of writing books. Using scientific research, Pennebaker has constructed a writing program to deal with trauma and difficult situations that has dramatically changed people's lives—enhancing both their emotional and physical well-being. I myself have written my way to emotional and physical wellness the Pennebaker way.*

—Louise DeSalvo
author of *Writing as a Way of Healing* and *Crazy in the Kitchen*

Writing to Heal

to

Heal

~ A ~

Guided Journal for

Recovering from

Trauma & Emotional

Upheaval

JAMES W. PENNEBAKER, PH.D.

New Harbinger Publications, Inc.

Distributed in Canada by Raincoast Books

Copyright © 2004 by James W. Pennebaker
         New Harbinger Publications, Inc.
         5674 Shattuck Avenue
         Oakland, CA 94609

Cover design by Amy Shoup
Interior design by Michele Waters

ISBN-10 1-57224-365-1
ISBN-13 978-1-57224-365-1

New Harbinger Publications' website address: www.newharbinger.com

09   08   07

10 9 8 7 6 5 4 3 2

Contents

Preface

If you are currently living with a trauma or emotional upheaval of some kind, you have taken a courageous step by opening this book. You may be seeking a way to deal with this event so that you can move on with your life. Or you may be tempted to avoid thinking about the trauma altogether and to pretend that everything is fine. Some of your closest friends might want you to do that, as well. However, the reality is that you can't ignore a massive upheaval that is probably affecting every aspect of your life.

This workbook was written for people who are living with a trauma or some kind of emotional upheaval. It may have taken place in the distant past or you may be in the middle of it right now. It could be a single event or a long-term chronic problem. Whatever it is, you probably find yourself thinking, worrying, even dreaming about it far too much. Hopefully, some form of expressive writing as described in this book will help you to get past some of the conflict, stress, or pain that you are feeling.

There are dozens of workbooks, workshops, and self-help systems available for dealing with emotional upheavals. Some may be beneficial for you; others may not. Most of these systems were developed by therapists and counselors who work with clients on a day-to-day basis. I'm not one of these people. I'm a research psychologist who accidentally discovered the power of writing during an experiment I conducted in the mid-1980s. In that original study, people were asked to write about either a traumatic experience or a superficial event for four consecutive days, fifteen minutes a day. To my surprise, those who wrote about their traumas needed less medical attention in the following months than they had previously; and many said the writing had changed their lives. Ever since then I've been devoted to understanding the mysteries of emotional writing.

I still am not exactly certain how or when or why expressive writing is beneficial. Although it doesn't always work with all people who have faced—or are facing—a trauma, it has been a remarkably successful technique for a large number of individuals. My best advice is for you to adopt the mind-set of a scientist yourself when you are reading and working with this book.

To get a sense of how the expressive writing method works, read the first two chapters. The specific writing exercises are introduced in chapter 3. Try them out.

If you feel that the traditional writing exercise is beneficial, that's great. If it is not helpful, try some of the other techniques discussed in the later chapters. You are responsible for figuring out the best way to tackle your own demons. For example, some people like to write something once and then throw it away. Others prefer to write, rewrite, and then rewrite their story again and again, editing and altering the story over time.

There is no absolute or correct way either to write about or to get past an emotional upheaval. Use this book as a rough guide. Stick with what works and drop what doesn't. Above all, trust your own intuition to recognize whether you are going in the right direction.

This workbook is based on the research of hundreds of researchers in psychology, medicine, anthropology, linguistics, and other intellectual disciplines. I have tried to be faithful to the findings of the scientific community and, at the same time, I have relied on my own intuition and experience in suggesting ways to approach expressive writing. Over the past two decades, thousands of people participated in experiments that have led us to a better understanding of the links between writing and health. Their willingness to tell their stories was the foundation for this work. It is to these volunteers that I dedicate this book.

—James W. Pennebaker
Austin, Texas

~ Part I ~

The Essentials of Writing

~ Chapter 1 ~

Why Write about Trauma or Emotional Upheaval?

What is the best way to get over a trauma? Over the last century researchers have been tackling this problem in many ways with varying success. For example, in-depth psychotherapy and medication have helped millions of people. Relaxation techniques including yoga and meditation have also proved beneficial. Strenuous exercise and improved eating habits can also help. Some of these strategies work for some people some of the time.

The reality, however, is that there is no one technique that is guaranteed to work. Since the mid-1980s, an increasing number of studies have focused on the value of expressive writing as a way to bring about healing. The evidence is mounting that the act of writing about traumatic experience for as little as fifteen or twenty minutes a day for three or four days can produce measurable changes in physical and mental health. Emotional writing also can affect people's sleeping habits, work efficiency, and how they connect to others. Indeed, when we put our traumatic experiences into words, we tend to become less concerned with the emotional events that have been weighing us down.

The purpose of this chapter is to convince you that expressive writing may be a potentially effective method for you to deal with a trauma or another emotional upheaval. The research evidence is indeed promising.

Perhaps you aren't interested in the scientific story behind expressive writing, or maybe you don't need convincing. If you want to skip the logic, and you are ready to jump in and try it, go directly ahead to chapter 2. If, however, like me, you are skeptical of any new method that purports to help people cope with traumatic experiences, read on. It may be helpful for you to learn how expressive writing has been tested, when and with whom it works, and when it has not produced compelling results.

Emotional Writing: A Brief History

At the outset, it's only fair to warn you that I am not a completely objective source about the power of expressive writing. I'm a researcher, not a therapist. In the late 1970s and early 1980s, I investigated traumatic experiences—all types of traumas—death of spouses, natural disasters, sexual traumas of all kinds, divorce, physical abuse, the Holocaust.

The scientific community had known for years that any kind of trauma is highly stressful. Researchers knew that after emotional upheavals, people are likely to become depressed or ill, experience changes in body weight and sleeping habits, and even die of heart disease and cancer at higher rates than the nontraumatized population. When my students and I studied the aftereffects of trauma, we found the same results.

We also found something more striking. Having a traumatic experience was certainly bad in many ways. But those people who had a trauma and kept that experience secret were much worse off. We learned that not talking to others about a trauma placed people at an even higher risk for major and minor illness compared to those who did talk about their traumas.

The dangers of keeping secrets were most apparent for major life traumas. In a series of surveys, several hundred college students and people who worked at a large corporation were asked to complete a brief questionnaire about traumas that had occurred earlier in their lives. The respondents were asked if prior to the age of seventeen they had experienced the death of a family member, the divorce of their parents, a sexual trauma, physical abuse, or some other event that had "changed their personality." For each item, they were also queried as to whether they had talked to anyone in detail about their experience.

Three of the striking results are apparent in figure 1. First, over half of the people we surveyed reported having experienced a major trauma in their life before the age of seventeen. Keep in mind that these were generally middle- and upper-middle class students and adults. Second, the people who had had any kind of major trauma before the age of seventeen visited their physicians for their illnesses at twice the rate of those who had not had a trauma. Finally, among those who had experienced traumas, those who had kept their traumas secret went to physicians almost 40 percent more often than those who had openly discussed their traumas (Pennebaker and Susman 1988).

Later research projects from many other labs confirmed these results. Adults whose spouses had committed suicide or had died suddenly in car accidents were healthier in the year following their spouse's death if they had

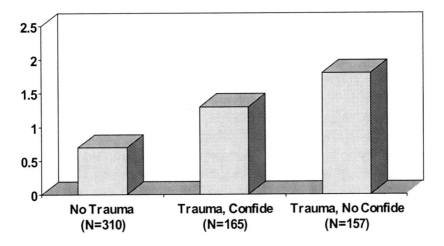

Figure 1: Number of physician visits for illness per year among people who report never having had a childhood trauma (No Trauma), having had one or more traumas about which they confided (Trauma, Confide), or having had at least one significant childhood trauma that they had kept secret (Trauma, No Confide).

talked about the trauma than those who had not discussed it. Gays and lesbians who had openly disclosed their sexual status, i.e., were out of the closet, were found to have fewer major health problems than gays and lesbians who had kept their sexual orientation a secret (Cole, Kemeny, Taylor, et al. 1996). Not talking about the important issues in life poses a significant health risk.

These original findings about the effect of keeping traumas secret led to the first expressive writing study. If not talking was potentially unhealthy, was it possible that asking people to talk, or even write, about their emotional upheavals could produce health improvements? In the mid-1980s, we tested this idea directly. Almost fifty students participated in the first writing project. They were reasonably healthy, ordinary young adults, most of whom had just started college. When they signed up for the experiment, they knew that they would be writing for fifteen minutes a day for four consecutive days. The only thing they didn't know was what their writing topics would be. Depending on the flip of a coin, students were asked to write about either emotional and traumatic topics or superficial, nonemotional topics.

Because this turned out to be a life-changing experiment for some of the participants (as well as for me), it might be helpful for you to think about what it was like for the people in this study. Imagine that you were escorted into my office and you were told the following:

> You have signed up for an experiment where you will write for fifteen minutes per day for four consecutive days. Everything you write will be anonymous and confidential. You will never receive any feedback

about your writing. At the conclusion of each day's writing, we ask that you put your writing into a large box so that we can analyze it. However, giving it to us is completely up to you. If you choose not to give it to us, you need not.

In your writing, I want you to really let go and explore your very deepest thoughts and feelings about the most traumatic experience of your life. You might try to tie this traumatic experience to other parts of your life: your childhood, your relationships with your parents, close friends, lovers, or any other people who are important to you. You might link your writing to your future and who you would like to become, to who you were in the past, or to who you are now. The important thing is for you to really let go and write about your deepest emotions and thoughts. You can write about the same thing all four days or about different things on each day; that is entirely up to you. Many people have never had traumatic experiences, but all of us have faced major conflicts or stressors, and you can write about those as well.

Many students were stunned by these instructions. Previously, virtually no one had ever encouraged them to write about some of the most significant experiences of their lives. Nevertheless, they went into their cubicles and wrote their hearts out. In this study, as in every study I have run since, people wrote about truly horrible experiences in their lives: terrible stories about divorce, rape, physical abuse, suicide attempts, and strange, quirky events that could never be categorized. Many students came out of their writing room in tears. Clearly, it was an emotionally trying experience for them. But they kept coming back. And, by the last day of the experiment, most reported that the experience had been profoundly important for them.

The real test was what would happen to these people in the weeks and months after they finished four days of expressive writing. With their permission, we were able to track their visits to physicians due to illness both before and after the study. Across our first four studies, those in the expressive writing groups made 43 percent fewer doctor visits for illness than the control group who wrote only about superficial topics. Most of the visits were for colds, flu, and other upper respiratory infections. Nevertheless, writing about personal traumas resulted in people visiting doctors for health reasons at half their normal rate (Pennebaker and Beall 1986).

If you like graphs and are not very critical, you might get excited about the results shown in figure 2. But it's important to put these effects into perspective. These are statistical findings based on four studies with relatively healthy college students. They don't tell us who may have benefited and who did not. They say nothing about why, when, and under what conditions expressive writing might work. Most important, they are not very helpful in answering the question, "Would writing about your emotions help you to deal with your life?"

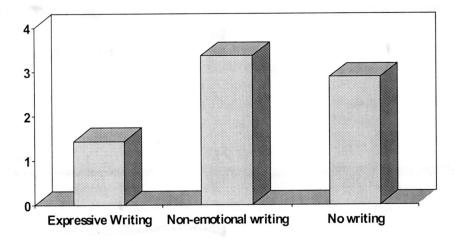

Figure 2: Yearly number of physician visits for illness in the three months after the experiment for participants in the emotional writing and control (non-emotional writing) groups. The No Writing data is based on students who did not participate in the experiment.

What Are the Effects of Writing?

Since the first expressive writing studies in the 1980s, dozens of similar experiments have been conducted. The first studies focused almost exclusively on physician visits for illness. As the number of studies increased, it became clear that writing was a far more powerful tool for healing than anyone had ever imagined. Only now, twenty years later, are we beginning to appreciate its potential impact.

Biological Effects

We know that people visit their doctors less after engaging in expressive writing. Are there also biological changes as a result of the writing? Yes, and the effects generalize across several physiological systems.

THE IMMUNE SYSTEM. The body's immune system can function more or less effectively depending on the person's stress level. Laboratories at Ohio State, the University of Miami, Auckland Medical School in New Zealand, and elsewhere have found that emotional writing is associated with general enhancement in immune function (Lepore and Smyth 2002). *Caution:* We don't really know what these effects mean in terms of long-term health.

MEDICAL HEALTH MARKERS. For their patients with chronic health problems, physicians often focus on specific indicators to determine whether the disease is being kept in check or getting worse. In recent years, researchers have found that emotional writing is associated with better lung function among asthma patients and lower pain and disease severity among arthritis sufferers (Smyth, Stone, Hurewitz, et al., 1999), higher white blood cell counts among AIDS patients (Petrie, Fontanilla, Thomas, et al. In press), and less sleep disruption among patients with metastatic cancers (De Moor, Sterner, Hall, et al., 2002). Other studies with relatively healthy adults have found modest reduction in resting blood pressure levels (Crow 2000) and liver enzyme levels often associated with excessive drinking (Francis and Pennebaker 1992).

PHYSIOLOGICAL INDICATORS OF STRESS. Somewhat surprisingly, while people are writing or talking about traumas, they often show immediate signs of reduced stress. For example, they demonstrate lower muscle tension in their faces and drops in the perspiration levels on their hands (often used in lie detection to measure the stress of deception). Immediately after writing about emotional topics, people evidence lower blood pressure and heart rate levels (Pennebaker, Hughes, and O'Heeron 1987).

Psychological Effects

The psychological and emotional effects of expressive writing are a bit more complicated than we had originally thought. It's important to distinguish between the immediate and long-term effects.

ONE'S MOOD CHANGES IMMEDIATELY AFTER WRITING. Feeling sad is normal. Immediately after writing about traumatic topics, people often feel worse. They get sad, even weepy. These effects are generally short term and last only for an hour or two. Emotional writing can be likened to seeing a sad movie; afterward you feel sadder but wiser. Being aware of this effect is extremely important. If you plan to write about important events in your life, be sure to allow yourself some time after writing to reflect.

LONG-TERM MOOD CHANGES. Expressive writing may make you sad for a brief time after doing it, but the long-term effects are surely worth the momentary sadness. People who engage in expressive writing report feeling happier and less negative than before writing. Similarly, reports of depressive symptoms, rumination, and general anxiety tend to drop in the weeks and months after writing about emotional upheavals (Lepore 1997).

Behavioral Changes

Writing does much more than affect your physical and mental health. You may start acting differently.

PERFORMANCE AT SCHOOL OR WORK. Among beginning college students, expressive writing helps them to adjust better to their new worlds.

Several studies have found that students make higher grades in the semester following a writing study (Cameron and Nicholls 1998; Lumley and Provenzano 2003; Pennebaker, Colder, and Sharp 1990). This may be due to the fact that emotional writing boosts working memory. *Working memory* is the technical term for our general ability to think about complex tasks. If we are worrying about things—including emotional upheavals in the past, we have less working memory. Expressive writing frees working memory, thus allowing us to deal with more complicated issues in our lives (Klein and Boals 2001).

DEALING WITH YOUR SOCIAL LIFE. Working with other people can sometimes be a daunting psychological task. The more emotional stress you are under, the more draining it can be to work with others. Recent studies have suggested that expressive writing can enhance the quality of people's social lives. In an attempt to explore this facet of writing about trauma, people were asked to wear a small tape recorder in the days before and after the writing so the researchers could monitor their social lives. Overall, those who wrote about their traumatic experiences talked more with others, laughed more easily and often, and used more words associated with positive emotions in the weeks afterward. Expressive writing seemed to make them more socially comfortable, better listeners, talkers, indeed, better friends (Pennebaker and Graybeal 2001).

Expressive writing may also be a method to alleviate anger and to make people more employable. A few years ago, I collaborated on a project with middle-aged men who had unexpectedly been laid off from their hi-tech jobs after working for the same company for over fifteen years. As a group, this was the most angry, hostile, unpleasant bunch I've ever worked with. Some of the participants were asked to write about their deepest emotions and thoughts about losing their jobs; the control group wrote about how they used their time (part of America's peculiar obsession with time management).

Eight months after writing, 52 percent of the emotional writing group had new jobs compared with only 20 percent of the time-management participants. Individuals from the two groups went to the same number of job interviews. The only difference was that the expressive writers were offered jobs (Spera, Buhrfeind, and Pennebaker 1994).

In many ways, the layoff study speaks to the heart of this workbook. Here was a group of successful men whose lives unexpectedly fell apart on a cold January day. The job market was terrible. Most of the men had families to support all while having to deal with the humiliation of losing their jobs. Most couldn't talk about their experience in any detail with their families, neighbors, or friends. Prior to the study, the few who had gone on job interviews had been so full of hostility that their interviewers had wanted nothing to do with them.

Only those men who were asked to address their emotions in writing benefited from the exercise. The writing helped them get past the experience. In the months after writing, when they went to job interviews , they were undoubtedly more at ease. They weren't compelled to tell their prospective employers how they had been abused by their last company. Expressive writing helped transform these men from hostile ruminators into more open-minded and accepting adults.

Who Benefits from Writing? Who Doesn't?

Although a great deal of effort has been devoted to creating a profile of the successful writer, the research has met with only limited success. In any given study, some but not all of the participants benefit. Here is what we know so far.

The Writer's Personality, Gender, Hostility, Emotional Awareness

The reality is that all types of people can benefit from writing about emotions. The personality differences that have been found have been remarkably subtle. One barely detectable difference, however, is the writer's gender. Across a large number of studies, males tend to benefit slightly more than females. In addition, people who tend to be naturally hostile and aggressive, as well as out of touch with their own emotions, show more health improvements after writing compared with their more easy-going, self-reflective, and open counterparts (Smyth 1998; Christensen, Edwards, Wiebe, et al. 1996).

Hostile, out-of-touch men may be particularly good candidates for expressive writing because they are the least likely to open up and talk with others. The more you can be yourself with your friends, the more likely you are to work through emotional upheavals. Keep in mind, however, that even the most emotionally expressive and open person in the world can sometimes get in a situation where he or she can't talk about a trauma or upheaval. In that case, writing can likely help.

EDUCATION OR WRITING ABILITY. Expressive writing studies have been conducted with people of widely varying educational levels and/or writing abilities. In some studies, the participants had no conception of spelling or grammar. It made no difference. They still told compelling and powerful stories. I have worked with people who were so severely punished during the course of their education that they were almost afraid to put anything into words for fear that I would rap their knuckles with a ruler. Once they appreciated that their writing would not be graded, judged, or linked to them, their anxiety disappeared.

RECENCY AND TYPE OF TRAUMA. How recently a trauma occurred probably *is* important. Although there has not been any systematic research on this, there is good reason to believe that expressive writing is probably not beneficial if the trauma occurred in the last few days. Depending on the severity of the trauma, people are often disoriented in the first one to three weeks after its occurrence. If you feel as though you are still reeling from a traumatic experience, then it is probably too early to start serious writing.

In terms of the type of trauma, we haven't found any differences in terms of the potential benefits. Some researchers believe that the more unexpected and unwanted the upheaval, the more likely that expressive writing will yield positive effects. One research group from a small town in Holland claims that writing about the natural death of a close friend or family member brings no benefits. However, they also claim that it causes no harm (Stroebe, Stroebe, Zech, et al. 2002).

CULTURE, CLASS, AND LANGUAGE. Positive effects have been found for expressive writing in countries around the globe: United States, Japan, New Zealand, Mexico, Holland, Germany, Spain, England, Hungary, and Poland. Writing in any language appears to work—whether it is done in the person's native language or not. Similarly, people can be from the upper, middle, or lower social classes in these countries and expressive writing continues to bring benefits to them (Lepore and Smyth 2002; Pennebaker 1997).

Do Certain Ways of Writing Work Better than Others?

One of the main debates in the expressive writing world these days concerns how and why it works. In an attempt to answer this question, we have gradually discovered that some ways of framing the writing technique are more effective than others. Some of these variations are introduced in some of the writing exercises in the second part of this workbook.

Writing versus Talking

Does talking about a trauma work as well as writing about it? It depends. One study compared talking about a trauma into a tape recorder with writing. Both techniques were equally beneficial (Esterling, Antoni, Fletcher, et al. 1994). Talking to someone about a trauma is far more complex than writing about it. To the degree the other person accepts you no matter what you say, and you can be completely honest in your disclosure, then talking may be more effective than writing. But there's the rub. If the person you confide in does not react favorably to you and to what you have to say, then talking may actually be worse for you than not confiding at all.

What about writing and then reading what you have written to someone else? Same problem. If your audience doesn't react ideally to what you say, you may come away with even more negative feelings. The only study that found negative effects for emotional writing required trauma patients to write about their traumas and then read their stories to other people in a group. Contrary to the researchers' expectations, this public reading made the patients more depressed (Gidron, Peri, Connolly, et al. 1996).

Safety in Writing

The role of an audience. People usually don't talk about emotional upheavals because they fear others' reactions. The purpose of expressive writing is for you to be completely honest and open with *yourself*. Your audience is you and you alone. When people describe the details of a trauma to someone they don't know or trust, they often hold back. If they can't tell their story honestly and completely, they don't get the full benefit of expressive writing.

Unlike every paper you wrote in school, expressive writing doesn't need to be read by anyone. In a study in our lab several years ago (Pennebaker 1997), we asked students to write about a trauma either on regular paper or on a child's Magic Pad. (Remember Magic Pads? You write on a sheet of gray plastic, and when you lift the sheet, all the writing disappears.) The same benefits accrued.

Writing Style

Some ways of writing appear to work better than others. Recent studies are converging on some common guidelines. People tend to benefit most from expressive writing if they follow the principles outlined below:

ACKNOWLEDGE YOUR EMOTIONS OPENLY. Emotional experiences are essential parts of a trauma. The ability to feel and label both the negative *and* the positive feelings that took place during and after the trauma is important.

CONSTRUCT A COHERENT STORY. Immediately after a trauma, everything often seems out of control and disconnected. One goal of emotional writing is to begin to put things back together again. One way to accomplish this is to work to make a meaningful story of what happened and how it is affecting you.

SWITCH PERSPECTIVES. People who have experienced a trauma initially see and understand it from only one perspective—their own. Indeed, when individuals begin to write about a massive upheaval, they first describe what they saw, felt, and experienced. Recent studies find that the people who benefit the most from expressive writing gradually begin to view the events of their trauma through others' eyes (Campbell and Pennebaker 2003).

FIND YOUR VOICE. A guiding principle of writing is that you must express yourself openly and honestly. People who write in a cold, detached manner and who quote Shakespeare, Aristotle, or Henry Ford may be fine historians and may even write great editorials in the local newspaper. But impressive writing is not the point of expressive writing. Those who benefit from writing the most are able to find a voice that reflects who they are.

WRITING BY HAND OR TYPING. Many people intuitively think that writing longhand is probably more beneficial than typing. Indeed, it is slower and allows them more time to think about what they are writing. The few studies that have examined these different ways of writing have not found any large or significant differences (Brewin and Lennard 1999). Most researchers would probably recommend that you write using whatever mode you find most comfortable.

Some Potential Dangers of Expressive Writing

So far, the way that expressive writing has been portrayed has made it sound like the world's greatest cure-all. Start writing today and you will get a new job, your health will improve, and you will be loved and admired by everyone. This sounds too good to be true. It is. There are both some imagined and real dangers to expressive writing that are often not appreciated.

A Minor Concern: Losing Control

In some quarters, there is the belief that traumatized people are barely holding onto their sanity. The fear is that even mentioning something upsetting can cause trauma victims to flip out. An extension of this type of thinking is that if people are asked to write about emotional upheavals, a certain proportion will start screaming and ranting uncontrollably.

I suppose it could happen. However, in the thousands of people I have observed working with expressive writing, it hasn't happened yet. On a few occasions, people have cried and became very sad. On three occasions in the last twenty years, we had to take people to see a psychologist. But all three wanted to return to the study the next day.

As will be discussed in greater detail in chapter 2, we instituted the Flip-Out Rule for our research and workshops. It's a very simple rule. If you fear that you might get too upset while writing about a particular topic, don't write about it. If you think that something will cause you to flip out, write about something else. This very simple rule works.

A Minimal Concern: Overanalyzing and Navel Gazing

Self-reflective writing should be viewed as a course-correction mechanism. If you are dealing with a traumatic experience, it is important to analyze it, try to understand it, and to get on with life. Occasionally, people will begin to reflect on an emotional upheaval and become completely obsessed with it. Their four-day writing procedure expands to forty days and then to 4,000 days. Frequently, they begin telling the same stories over and over, never finding any resolution.

There is convincing evidence that suggests writing about the same topic in the same way day after day is not at all helpful, in fact, it may be harmful. You *can* analyze something too much. If, after several days of writing, you feel that you are not making any progress, then you need to rethink your writing strategy. Try some of the other approaches you will find in this book. If that doesn't seem to work, consider talking to a professional: a therapist, social worker, minister, or to a trustworthy friend.

A Moderate Concern: Blackmail and Humiliation

In the literature about child abuse, one of the most troubling events concerns instances where children tell their mothers or fathers about sexual abuse and the parents either don't believe them or blame them for causing it. The evidence suggests that in many such cases these children would have been better off keeping their abuse secret.

What if you write about your deepest emotions and thoughts and someone reads your journal? Over the years, I have heard of many instances where a spouse, parent, or a friend read someone's diary and it changed their relationship forever, often in a bad way. Your writing must be private and for you alone. If there is a possibility that someone will read your expressive writing entries, then you must come up with a way to hide or destroy them. It is bad enough dealing with major emotional upheavals in your life. You don't need anyone else judging you about your experiences.

A Serious Concern: Potential Life Changes

We live our lives in a web of connections. Changing one aspect of our lives has the potential to affect many others. The ways you deal with your trauma may be exactly what your friends and family desire most. If you change your coping strategies, you might affect your closest relationships in ways you never imagined. Two stories illustrate this problem.

Two Stories

Several years ago, I worked with a young woman whose husband had died suddenly almost a year earlier. Through her coworkers I learned that she was viewed as a pillar of strength; she had been happy, courageous, even inspirational in her optimism in the wake of her loss. She came to me because she felt she needed to write about her husband's death, which she did. By the last day of writing, she was transformed. She was more relaxed, her blood pressure was lower, and she was deeply appreciative about the writing experience.

Two months later, we met to discuss her life and the writing intervention. In the interim, she had quit her job, stopped seeing her friends at work, and had moved back to her hometown. She said that all of those changes were the result of the writing. Because of the writing experience, she had realized she was on a life path she no longer wanted. She was putting up a false, cheerful front for her friends and she discovered that the only people she could be truly honest with were her childhood friends.

Was expressive writing good for her? Some would say that it undermined her career, her financial future, and her entire social network. She maintained it was a lifesaver.

The second case is even more striking. A woman in her early forties with three children told me of her need to write in order to deal with a series of terrible childhood events that haunted her. After several days of writing, she reported that she felt free for the first time in her life. Over the next few months, however, she left her husband and, with her children, she moved into low-income housing where she barely eked out a living. She went through a period of deep, almost suicidal depression from which she gradually escaped.

In a recent interview with her, she maintained that the writing was the direct cause of her divorce, depression, and poverty. But like the woman whose husband died, she is also grateful for the writing she did and the insights she gained. She said that deep down she knew she had to address some of the basic issues from her past that had been causing her profound unhappiness and conflict. The cost was higher than she had anticipated, but in retrospect, she thought it had been worth it.

These two cases suggest that writing can be a significant threat. By reducing your inner conflicts, you may affect the course of your life and the lives of others in unintended ways. Statistically, we have found that most people report that the life changes following emotional writing are beneficial. Indeed, even these two individuals whose lives were so deeply changed are appreciative of the power of this kind of writing.

Nothing is as simple as it seems.

> *The unexamined life is not worth living*
> —Socrates

> *This above all: to thine ownself be true,*
> *And it must follow, as the night the day,*
> *Thou canst not then be false to any man.*
> —William Shakespeare (*Hamlet*)

~ Chapter 2 ~

Getting Ready to Write

In the next chapter, a basic writing exercise is outlined. This four-day writing approach has proven effective for improving mental and physical health. What the simple writing instructions don't convey is the power of your *writing context*. Where, when, and how you write can sometimes be as important as what you write.

This chapter will help you set the stage for your writing. Indeed, think of writing as a form of ritual. For it to have maximal effect, it's best to do your writing in a meaningful place, time, and atmosphere. As you begin setting up the context for your writing, it is also important to begin contemplating what your writing topic should be.

What to Write

On its surface, this workbook is for people dealing with emotional upheavals or traumas. What is perplexing about traumas, however, is that directly or indirectly they influence every part of your life. In the context of this workbook, this means that you might start writing about a clear, unambiguous traumatic experience but then find yourself writing about something entirely different. For example, I have seen many instances where people start writing about the death of a parent as their traumatic experience and, within fifteen minutes, they are devoting most of their energy dealing with their marital issues. That's okay. Here are some simple guidelines.

START WITH AN EMOTIONAL UPHEAVAL THAT IS BOTHERING YOU. In most cases, this is quite straightforward. You know why you are having sleep problems, why you keep thinking about the upheaval. Begin writing about the upheaval, but if you find yourself moving to another topic, go with it.

TRUST WHERE YOUR WRITING TAKES YOU. You may start off with a trauma but soon find yourself writing about other topics. As long as these other topics are emotionally important, follow them. If, however, you find yourself writing about what you would like for dinner, or some other distracting topic, then force yourself back to the trauma. Also, if you find yourself getting bored with your trauma writing, switch topics. Ask yourself what emotional topics have been keeping you awake at night or that you have been actively avoiding.

LET SLEEPING DOGS LIE. We have all had painful experiences that we have had to deal with. We no longer think about them and they don't appear to affect us in any way. If dredging up these old issues aren't relevant to your life right now, why write about them?

DEAL ONLY WITH TRAUMAS OF WHICH YOU ARE AWARE. There is a remarkable literature dealing with repressed memories. One of the main concepts explored in that literature is the idea that many people had horrible childhood experiences that they don't remember, many of which involved childhood sexual abuse. If you have no memory of a given childhood experience, go with the working assumption that it never happened. Write only about traumas and upheavals stored in your consciousness. This may save you thousands of dollars in therapy and legal bills.

How Often to Write

Virtually every study conducted with expressive writing asked people to write for about fifteen or twenty minutes a day for only three or four consecutive days. For the purpose of this workbook, that's all that I'm requesting as well. Promise yourself that you will try expressive writing for four days. That's all. If you want to write more, then do it. If you want to try some other writing exercises suggested in the later chapters in the book, great. But to determine whether expressive writing can be helpful to you, use chapter 3 as a guide and set aside the time to write for twenty minutes each day for four days.

CONSECUTIVE WRITING DAYS? There is some debate about whether it is better to write for four consecutive days or to separate the days. One study, for example, reported that it might be better to write once a week for four consecutive weeks (Smyth 1998). Your schedule and the urgency you feel in dealing with any emotional upheavals you are living with is part of the issue. My own experience is that writing for four consecutive days is a bit more efficient.

THE TWENTY-MINUTE MINIMUM. What if you want to keep writing after twenty minutes? Then keep on writing. The twenty-minute rule is an arbitrary minimum. That is, plan to write for at least twenty minutes each day with the understanding that you can write more but shouldn't write less.

THE FOUR-DAY MINIMUM. What if you find that you enjoy writing and want to continue past the four days? Do it. Many people find that once they begin writing they have a large number of issues that they need to think and write about. Write for as many days as you need; just think of the four days as a minimum.

KEEPING A DAILY JOURNAL: GOOD IDEA OR BAD? Ironically, there is no clear evidence that keeping a daily journal or diary is good for your health. One reason might be that once people get into the habit of writing every day, they devote less and less time to dealing with important psychological issues. My own experience is that journal writing works best when used on an as-needed basis. If your life is going well, you are happy, and you are not obsessing about anything in the past, why overanalyze yourself? Let it go and enjoy life as it comes. It is safe to say that some future miseries will come to visit you again. When they do, do some writing to deal with them.

BOOSTER WRITING SESSIONS. Think of expressive writing as a tool that will always be at your disposal. It is like having medicine in your medicine cabinet. There is no need to take the medicine when you are healthy, but when you are under the weather, you can always turn to it. Once you have tried writing as a healing agent, try it again when you need to. Also, you might find that in the future, you won't need to write for four days, twenty minutes a day. Merely writing occasionally when something bothers you might be sufficient.

When to Write: Questions about Time

Let's not get too philosophical here, but there are many issues about time that must be addressed, from the time of your life to the time of day.

Time After a Trauma

Traumas and emotional upheavals can be tricky. Some happen quickly and end abruptly. Others never seem to end. When deciding to write, consider the following issues:

A Recent Trauma

If you have faced a massive traumatic experience in your life within the last two to three weeks, it may be too early for you to write about it. At the very least, it may be too soon for you to deal with some of the deeper emotions that the trauma has awakened. If the trauma or emotional upheaval is too raw, begin your writing in a relatively safe way, perhaps by describing what is happening in your life right now. As you begin feeling more comfortable, you can start dealing with the trauma and its effects more deeply. If you don't feel as though you are ready to write, then don't. Come back to this book in a few weeks.

An Ongoing Emotional Upheaval

Some traumas and emotional upheavals have a life of their own: they are always around in one form or another. Some examples include living with a fatal or chronic disease, going through a divorce, dealing with an abusive parent or spouse. The list could be endless. For situations like these, writing has been found to be beneficial. You might find that writing for four days now makes a big difference. However, as your trauma or emotional event unfolds in the future, additional writing may be helpful as well.

A Trauma in the Past

The original writing technique was designed for people who had experienced a traumatic experience in the past. It could have been a month or decades ago. Writing is particularly recommended if you find yourself thinking, worrying, or dreaming about the event frequently. Expressive writing can also help if you find that this upheaval is adversely affecting your daily life in some way.

A Trauma in the Future

Can it be helpful to write about the eventual death of a loved one? Or a divorce that you know is coming? Or something else coming into view in the future? Sure, why not. It's free. But in your writing, explore why you are feeling the way that you are and how these feelings relate to other issues in your life.

Is This a Good Time in Your Life to Write?

Expressive writing can force you to deal with important emotional experiences that you may have been avoiding. Oftentimes, people brainstorm and talk with others about these events in some detail over the course of writing. There may be certain times in your life when you can afford the time to deal with emotional upheavals better than other times. All things being equal, if you have the luxury of choosing your writing time, the following times would be preferable:

~ When it is a slow time for you at work

~ When you are on vacation

~ When it is the beginning of a weekend

~ When you are not inundated with other tasks

~ When you have some time to yourself after each day's writing to engage in self-reflection

Unfortunately, emotional upheavals often come along at inconvenient times. They also have the nasty habit of creating inconvenience. Consequently, you may have to write expressively at a time in your life that feels hectic and out of control. And that's far better than not writing at all.

Choosing a Time of Day to Write

I'm a big believer in trying to write at the same time every day if at all possible. Part of the reason for this is to establish a regular writing ritual. To the degree that this is possible, it is critical to consider what you will be doing after each day's writing. At least two studies have suggested that people need some reflection time after their writing (Petrie, Booth, and Pennebaker 1998). That is, you don't want to set up your writing so that as soon as you finish, you must immediately go to an important business meeting.

In her very popular book *The Artist's Way* (2002), Julia Cameron suggests that people can greatly benefit from doing relatively unstructured writing exercises every morning as soon as they wake up. In her view, this is a good way to clear the mind before beginning the day. Although I'm not familiar with any research that supports this idea, my intuition is that it makes good sense. Writing about a traumatic experience in the morning may work as well as any other time depending on what you do after writing. If you have some free time afterward, then this might be a good time to do it.

Across multiple studies, we have had most success with people writing at the end of their workday. If you have children and need to tend to them in the evening, after they have gone to bed might be a good time to write. The important rule, however, is for you to have some free time after writing to let your mind reflect on what you have written.

Where to Write

Consider the construction of healing environments. Most physicians' offices and hospitals exhibit common layouts, odors, lighting, and uniforms. Once you enter one of these places, there is a subtle sense of cleanliness, order, structure, and, yes, physical healing. Churches, temples, and mosques all have their own unique environments as well. As you enter them, you often can feel your body relax and change.

Think of the expressive writing method as your own healing ritual. Because you are your own physician (or priest or goddess), you get to create your own setting. Based on my research with expressive writing, certain suggestions come to mind:

Create a Unique Environment

It's ideal to have a place for your writing where, typically, you don't work. If your living arrangement is such that you can't get any privacy, go to a library, religious establishment, coffee house, or even outside to a park. Wherever you go to write should be a place that provides you with a sense of comfort and security.

Most people prefer to write at home. If you have a special room where you can write, set it up so that it is a little different than usual. Change the lighting, for example. In one series of studies, we covered lamps in the laboratory with red cellophane and put them on the floor to create odd shadows. We wanted to make the room look like no other.

Create a Ritual for Writing

As part of establishing a unique environment, think about setting up your room in the same way each day. You might consider lighting a candle when you begin writing and ceremoniously extinguishing it when you are finished. Some people use incense to create a distinctive smell. Others bring pictures or objects that have significance for them into their writing area as a way to symbolize the emotional event. Your ritual may begin before writing and extend to the time after writing. It is not uncommon for people to exercise or engage in meditation before or after writing each day. A long shower or bath before or after writing can become a cleansing ritual. Similarly, putting on a special cap, a particular blouse or shirt, or wearing nothing at all can be a signal for you to get into your writing. You are the boss. Create the environment or ritual best suited to your personality and your specific needs.

The Writing Tools

This workbook was designed for you to write in it. But you really don't have to. Some people prefer to buy their own journal book and others would rather write directly into a computer. Whether you write in this workbook or not makes no difference in terms of the value of writing. The value comes in doing the actual writing.

Many people want explicit instructions about the details of writing. Should you use a pen or pencil? Does color matter? It's up to you. Do you prefer writing with a pen? Then use a pen. Do you prefer a blue pencil? Ditto. Blood? It's up to you.

The Flip-Out Rule

I hereby declare you ready to begin your expressive writing experience. But before you start, it is important to review the Flip-Out Rule.

> *If you feel that your writing about a particular topic is too much for you to handle, then do not write about it. If you know that you aren't ready to address a particularly painful topic, write about something else. When you are ready, then tackle it. If you feel that you will flip out by writing, don't write.*

What could be simpler? Enjoy your writing.

~ Chapter 3 ~

The Basic Writing Technique

This chapter presents the essential features of the expressive writing method. The instructions have been drawn from dozens of successful writing studies. For your first exercise, your goal is to write a minimum of twenty minutes per day for four consecutive days. It's okay to skip days but the sooner you complete the four-day exercise, the better.

It is also recommended that after completing each day's writing that you answer the brief questionnaire. The questionnaire is a rough indicator of how the writing is affecting you. Once you have finished all four days of writing, you can go back and evaluate how your impressions have evolved over time. Chapter 4 will walk you through ways of analyzing and thinking about your writing samples.

General Instructions

For the next four days, you will be asked to write about a trauma or emotional upheaval that profoundly affected your life. There are a few simple guidelines to keep in mind while you are writing:

WRITE FOR TWENTY MINUTES A DAY. If you wind up writing for more than twenty minutes, that's great. Nevertheless, the following day you must write for a minimum of twenty minutes. You may not count any extra time spent writing one day to carry over to the next day.

WRITING TOPIC. You can write about the same event on all four days or about different events each day. Not everyone has had a major trauma that they want to write about. However, we have all had major conflicts or stressors in our lives that you can also write about. However, whatever you choose to write about should be something that is extremely personal and important for you.

WRITE CONTINUOUSLY. Once you begin writing, write continuously without stopping. Don't worry about spelling or grammar. Your high school English teacher will never see it. If you run out of things to say, simply repeat what you have already written.

WRITE ONLY FOR YOURSELF. You are writing for yourself and no one else. Plan to destroy or hide what you have written when you have finished. Do not turn this exercise into a letter. After you complete your expressive writing task, if you want to write a letter, then do it. But this exercise is for your eyes only.

THE FLIP-OUT RULE. If you feel as though you cannot write about a particular event because it will "push you over the edge," then don't write about it. Deal only with those events or situations that you can handle now. If you have additional traumatic topics that you can't get to now, you can always deal with them in the future.

WHAT TO EXPECT AFTER WRITING. Many people often feel somewhat saddened or depressed after expressive writing, especially on the first day or two of writing. If this happens to you, it is completely normal. The feeling usually lasts a few minutes or, in some cases, hours, much like going to a sad movie. If possible, plan to have some time to yourself after you end your expressive writing session to reflect on the issues you have been writing about.

Day 1: Writing Instructions

Remember that this is the first of four days of emotional writing. For today's work, your goal is to write about your deepest thoughts and feelings about the trauma or emotional upheaval that has been influencing your life the most. In your writing, really let go and explore the event and how it has affected you. For today, it may be beneficial simply to write about the event itself, how you felt when it was occurring, and how you feel about it now.

As you write about this event, you might begin to tie it to other parts of your life. For example, how is it related to your childhood and your relationships with your parents and close family members? How is it connected to those people you have most loved, feared, or been angry at? How is this upheaval related to your current life, your friends and family, your work, and your place in life? Above all, how is this event related to who you were in the past, who you would like to be in the future, and who you are now?

In today's writing, it is particularly important that you really let go and examine your deepest emotions and thoughts surrounding this upheaval in your life. Remember to write continuously the entire twenty minutes. And never forget that this writing is for you and you alone.

At the conclusion of your twenty minutes of emotional writing, read the section "Post-Writing Thoughts."

Day 1 Writing

Post-Writing Thoughts Following the Day 1 Writing Session

Congratulations, you have completed your first day of writing. Before putting down this workbook for the day, please complete the following questionnaire. Put a number between 0 and 10 by each question, where the numbers mean,

0	1	2	3	4	5	6	7	8	9	10
not at all					somewhat					a great deal

1. To what degree did you express your deepest thoughts and feelings? ____

2. To what degree do you currently feel sad or upset? ____

3. To what degree do you currently feel happy? ____

4. To what degree was today's writing valuable and meaningful for you? ____

5. In the space below, briefly describe how your writing went today:

For many people, the first day of expressive writing is the most difficult. This kind of writing can bring up emotions and thoughts that you may not have known you had. It also may have flowed much more easily than you had expected it to, especially if you wrote about something that you have been keeping to yourself for a long time.

If you are worried that someone will see your writing, you can tear out the actual writing pages from this workbook. You can keep the pages in a secure place or you can destroy them. If keeping them is not a problem, you may want to go back and analyze them at the end of the four days of writing.

Now, take some time for yourself. Until tomorrow.

Day 2: Writing Instructions

Today is the second day of the four-day expressive writing process. In your last writing session, you were asked to explore your thoughts and feelings about a trauma or emotional upheaval that affected you deeply. In today's writing, your task is to *really* examine your very deepest emotions and thoughts. You can write about the same trauma or upheaval as you did yesterday or a completely different one.

The writing instructions today are similar to those of your last writing session. In your writing, try to link the trauma to other parts of your life. It is important to realize that a trauma or an emotional upheaval often may influence every aspect of your life, from your relationships with friends and family, to how you view yourself and others view you, to your work, and even to how you think about your past. In today's writing, begin thinking how this trauma or upheaval is affecting your life in general. You might also write about how you may be responsible for some of the effects of the trauma. As before, write continuously for the entire twenty minutes and open up your deepest thoughts and feelings. At the conclusion of your writing, complete the post-writing questionnaire at the end of this section.

Day 2 Writing

Post-Writing Thoughts Following the Day 2 Writing Session

You have now completed the second of the four-day expressive writing process. Before putting down this book for the day, please complete the following questionnaire. Put a number between 0 and 10 beside each question, where the numbers mean,

0	1	2	3	4	5	6	7	8	9	10
not at all					somewhat					a great deal

1. To what degree did you express your deepest thoughts and feelings? ____

2. To what degree do you currently feel sad or upset? ____

3. To what degree do you currently feel happy? ____

4. To what degree was today's writing valuable and meaningful for you? ____

5. In the space below, briefly describe how your writing went today:

You now have two days of writing that you can begin to compare. How does today's writing compare with your first day's emotional writing? Did you notice that your topic shifted? How about the way you were writing? Between now and your next writing, think about what you have written. Are you starting to see things in a different light? How is writing affecting your emotions?

Now give yourself a little time to step back from your writing. Until tomorrow.

Day 3: Writing Instructions

You have now made it through two days of writing. After today's writing assignment, you will have only one more day of emotional writing to do. Tomorrow, then, you will need to wrap up your story. Today, however, it is important for you to continue to explore your deepest thoughts and emotions about the topics you have been tackling so far.

On the surface, today's writing assignment is very similar to the earlier assignments. You can focus on the same topics you have been examining or you can shift your focus either to another trauma or to some other feature of the same trauma. Your primary goal, however, is to focus on your emotions and thoughts about those events that are affecting your life the most right now.

It is important that you don't repeat what you have already written in the first two writing exercises. Writing about the same general topic is fine, but you also need to explore it from different perspectives and different points of view. As you write about this emotional upheaval, what are you feeling and thinking? How has this event shaped your life and who you are?

In today's writing, allow yourself to explore especially those deep issues about which you may be particularly vulnerable. As always, write continuously for the entire twenty-minute session.

Day 3 Writing

Post-Writing Thoughts Following the Day 3 Writing Session

You have completed the next-to-last day of writing. Please complete the following questionnaire using a number between 0 and 10 by each question, where the numbers mean,

	0	1	2	3	4	5	6	7	8	9	10
not at all						somewhat					a great deal

1. To what degree did you express your deepest thoughts and feelings? ____

2. To what degree do you currently feel sad or upset? ____

3. To what degree do you currently feel happy? ____

4. To what degree was today's writing valuable and meaningful for you? ____

5. In the space below, briefly describe how your writing went today:

In most studies, the third day of writing is highly significant. Some people get to some of the most critical issues that they have been avoiding. Whereas the first two writing sessions can be like dipping your toes in the water to see if it's too cold, by the third day some people are ready to jump completely in. A second group of people open up to emotional writing the most on the first day. By the third day of writing members of this group sometimes begin to run out of steam. Both patterns are associated with improved health.

As with your last writing exercise, try to compare what you have written across the three sessions. What issues are surfacing as most important for you? Have you been surprised by any of your feelings while you were writing? Has the writing provoked any new or important thoughts during the periods that you have been away from the workbook?

Remember that tomorrow is the final day of the four-day writing exercise. The instructions for your last assignment will be much like today's. Since it will be the final day, however, think about how you will tie up any loose ends.

Now pamper yourself a bit. Until tomorrow.

Day 4: Writing Instructions

This is the final day of the four-day writing exercise. As with the previous days' writings, you are to explore your deepest emotions and thoughts about those upheavals and issues in your life that are most important and troublesome for you. Stand back and think about the events, issues, thoughts, and feelings that you have disclosed. In your writing, try to tie up anything that you haven't yet confronted. What are your emotions and thoughts at this point? What have you learned, lost, and gained as a result of this upheaval in your life? How will these events from your past guide your thoughts and actions in the future?

Really let go in your writing and be honest with yourself about this upheaval. Do your best to wrap up the entire experience into a meaningful story that you can take with you into the future.

Day 4 Writing

Post-Writing Thoughts Following the Final Writing Session

You have now completed the last day of expressive writing. Please complete the following questionnaire using a number between 0 and 10 by each question, where the numbers mean,

```
        0    1    2    3    4    5    6    7    8    9    10
    not at all                somewhat              a great deal
```

1. To what degree did you express your deepest thoughts and feelings? ____

2. To what degree do you currently feel sad or upset? ____

3. To what degree do you currently feel happy? ____

4. To what degree was today's writing valuable and meaningful for you? ____

5. In the space below, briefly describe how your writing went today:

Today concludes the basic four-day writing exercise. Most people find the last day of writing the least enjoyable. If that is the case for you, this is often a sign that you are tired of dealing with this trauma and want to get on with some other aspects of your life.

In some ways, it may be tempting to go back over the various writing samples, questionnaire responses, and personal observations immediately after the fourth writing day. Indeed, it is important to do this. However, it is strongly recommended that you take at least two to three days off from the writing exercise. When you are ready to begin assessing your writing, turn to the next chapter.

~ Chapter 4 ~

Looking Back at Your Writing

Did the four-day writing exercise make a difference in your life? If so, it can be helpful to try to dissect which aspects were most helpful. By finding what may have helped the most, you can begin to structure your own writing exercises in the future to maximize the potential of expressive writing. If you feel that you did not gain any benefits from expressive writing, however, it is time to do some serious troubleshooting to see what might have gone wrong.

To get maximum benefit from this chapter, it is best to read it several days or even weeks after you have completed the four-day writing exercise. However, if you have just finished the writing and want to know more, go ahead and read the chapter now but come back to it after some time has elapsed. If you saved your writings, have them with you.

Measuring Change

Perhaps the reason I believe it's important to document any changes the writing may have brought about comes from my scientific side. In any case, I believe it is important to be aware of any changes you are undergoing. Compare how you felt and behaved in the last day or two with the days before you started writing. Have you noticed any of the following changes?

~ Feeling more positive emotions; easier to laugh

~ Falling asleep faster; better sleep in general

~ Feeling healthier, fewer aches and pains

~ Drinking less alcohol, taking fewer drugs, eating more healthily

~ Thinking about the trauma less and, when you do think about it, the thoughts are less painful

~ Feeling less irritable, fewer disagreements or fights with others (feeling the sense that other people seem nicer)

~ Creating more honest and open relationships with others

~ Focusing on work more easily; getting things done

~ Feeling a greater sense of meaning in your life; having a better understanding of the emotional upheaval you wrote about

These are some of the most common findings in the research literature on expressive writing. If you noticed changes in at least some of these feelings or behaviors, expressive writing is probably a good coping system for you. Indeed, you might find additional value in experimenting with other writing strategies that are outlined in the remainder of the book.

What if the writing made you feel worse rather than better? In a small percentage of cases, this happens and it is a normal reaction. If you feel that you are in particularly bad shape, experiencing feelings of deep depression, self-destructive thoughts, and engaging in potentially dangerous behaviors, you need to talk to someone. In the Resources section of this workbook you will find the phone numbers of a number of organizations that are available for crisis counseling.

If you didn't benefit from writing but still feel as though there might be some potential benefit in it for you, read the rest of this chapter. There may be some secrets that you can uncover in your writings that will help to guide you in the future.

Looking at the Writings

If you wrote longhand (rather than on a computer) and saved your writing samples, stand back and look at them as if you were a scientist who spoke no English. Start with your handwriting. Did the overall neatness of your writing change from day to day? How about the slant of your writing? Many people will see a change in their writing as they gradually deal with an upsetting experience.

Look at the handwriting of a woman who wrote for four days about a deeply upsetting sexual experience that happened to her when she was a young teenager. On the first day of expressive writing in describing the event, her handwriting was very controlled. But as she wrote more on the following days, her handwriting became more expressive. In many ways, the different ways she wrote mirrored the changes in her thinking about the event over time.

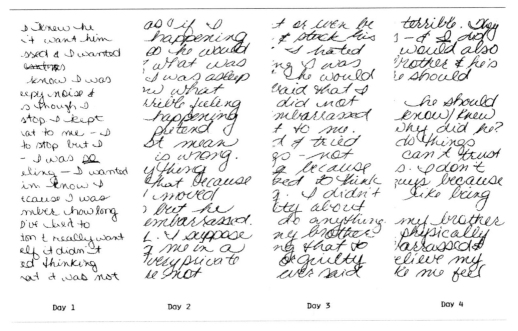

Figure 3: Handwriting sample of a twenty-one-year-old woman writing about the same emotional upheaval across the four-day writing exercise.

In addition to your handwriting, pay attention to strike-outs or erasures. When people are editing themselves, or trying to maintain a particular public image, it is common for them to edit themselves very carefully as they go along. Mark-outs and corrections also hint that the person is paying relatively more attention to how they are writing than to what they are writing.

Finally, there are an almost infinite number of other ways to analyze writing. Look at changes in spelling, the use of particular words, the pressure you were exerting on the paper as you were writing, change in punctuation, or even page layout from day to day. How do these stylistic changes correspond to the topics you were dealing with? Bear in mind that no one knows what all these changes might mean in revealing your psychological makeup. You, however, are the best detective to solve this puzzle.

Eyeing the Numbers

At the conclusion of each day's writing, you were given four brief questions about your writing. If you completed the questionnaire items, look back over them. The first question asked the degree to which you expressed your deepest emotions and thoughts for that day's writing. Using the 10-point scale, most people will mark an 8, 9, or 10 thus indicating that they were quite expressive in their writing. The one exception that we sometimes see occurs on the last day. Often, many people are psychologically finished with their writing on the last day; they can't get up the energy to delve as deeply into their thoughts and emotions to the same degree as on the previous days.

If you reported a number 5 or less across most of the writing days, what was going on with you? If you felt that writing was not particularly beneficial, you may not have expressed your emotions and thoughts enough.

The next questions asked the degree that you felt sad and happy after writing. Interestingly, most people feel relatively sad after writing, particularly on the first days of writing. However, they generally become less sad each day. This drop in sadness and a corresponding increase in happiness is a mark of the benefits to be had with expressive writing. You might also explore how the topics you addressed were related to your mood changes after writing. Did some topics affect you in ways that you weren't expecting?

In many ways, the last questionnaire item that you completed each day was the most important one. You were asked to evaluate the degree to which each day's writing was valuable and meaningful for you. If your numbers were consistently low (5 or lower), then you need to rethink how you approached the writing exercise. It may be that writing isn't a particularly helpful strategy for you. Alternatively, this type of writing may not be useful but other types could be. Be sure and read the next section before deciding what to do.

Analyzing Your Writings

Are some ways of writing more beneficial than others? This question is mystifying the research world these days. In theory, if we can find certain ways of writing that are the healthiest, we can prescribe them to people. Did you notice how little was said in the first part of this workbook on how to write? That's because the research community still hasn't figured out what works best.

However, there are some promising findings on the horizon. In the last few years, a number of researchers have analyzed the writing samples of people who benefited from writing as well as from people who did not benefit. Although the results are based on fairly esoteric linguistic analyses, they may have value for you in interpreting your own writing.

Expressing Emotions in Writing

Traumatic experiences, by their very nature, elicit powerful and complex emotions. We have known for a long time that people who do not or cannot refer to their own feelings when writing about a trauma tend not to benefit from the writing exercise.

USE NEGATIVE EMOTIONS IN MODERATION. More interesting, however, is the relative use of negative versus positive emotions in writing.

Traumas, of course, tend to be associated with a host of negative emotions: sadness, guilt, anger, anxiety, and depression. Not being able to express or acknowledge these real feelings can be a problem. Sometimes people don't express them because they were viewed as "unacceptable" emotions some time in their past. Having emotions is not a question of right or wrong—they just are. If you feel an emotion while writing about a trauma, admit it on paper.

The tricky aspect of negative emotions, however, is that they need to be acknowledged but not dwelt upon. Across multiple studies, those people who use the most negative emotion words (e.g., hate, cry, hurt, afraid) while writing about traumas tend not to benefit much from the writing experience. It may be that they are caught in a spiral of self-pity. Perhaps focusing so much on their negative feelings may blind people to some of the causes and consequences of an emotional upheaval. Finally, it also might be that excessive use of negative emotions when writing could be a signal that the writer is deeply depressed. Indeed, people who are profoundly depressed may not benefit from writing until their depression lifts. (Note: if you are deeply depressed, seek help. See the Resources section for some suggestions.)

POSITIVE EMOTIONS: THE MORE THE BETTER. Even the most horrendous life experiences can provide positive feelings and insights. In some circles, this is almost an heretical idea. This is not to say that traumas are good events—rather, their value lies in having the potential to remind us of the good things in life.

One of the most surprising findings about expressive writing is that the more that people can use positive emotions in their writing, the more they benefit from the exercise. We see positive emotions when words such as love, caring, funny, joy, beautiful, and warmth are used. The degree to which people can use these words even when they are dealing with terrible traumas predicts health improvements after writing.

Being able to acknowledge positive emotions when dealing with tragic events is related to work on optimism and benefit-finding. Across an increasing number of studies, people who are able to see the positive sides of negative experiences tend to cope better. This is not to say that you should be some kind of Pollyanna who pretends everything is wonderful. In fact, if you have tried to do this in the past, you probably learned that it doesn't work.

The take-home message from this research is that it is important to acknowledge the bad and look for the good. The degree to which you can do this in your writing is one factor that correlates with improved health.

Constructing a Story

Why would humans have evolved in such a way that expressive writing can be emotionally beneficial? Very likely, the answer can be found in the nature of language and human relationships. Since the beginning of spoken language, people have used words to describe events to others. Part of any description of an event is built around a story or narrative. If I tell you how I got a flat tire on my car, there is a standard way I'll describe the event: the setting of the scene, the occurrence of the unexpected event, my reaction to it, and what happened afterward.

Stories are an essential part of who we are. They provide a way for us to understand simple and extremely complicated experiences. Just as we need stories to convey ideas or events to others, so too do we need stories to understand the things that happen to us. One argument within the expressive writing world is that one of the major predictors of improved health is the authors' ability to construct a coherent story around the traumatic experience. There is some interesting evidence for this.

Certain types of words can serve as markers of stories. For example, causal words, such as cause, effect, because, reason, and rationale, suggest that the writer is conveying what may have caused what. Causal reasoning is a way of understanding an event. That is, if I know what caused it, I'll have a much better appreciation of when (or if) it might reoccur in the future. Similarly, another class of words, called insight words (including words like understand, realize, know, meaning) point to the person's standing back trying to formulate a broader understanding of an event or trauma.

Several studies have demonstrated that people who increase their use of these story-markers, causal, and insight words, tend to show the greatest improvements in physical health after expressive writing (Pennebaker, Mayne, and Francis 1997). What appears to be happening is that those who start off using a relatively low rate of these words and then increase their usage of these words over the days of writing are putting together a story about their trauma.

In thinking about the phrase "constructing a story," there should be an emphasis on the word *constructing*. Merely having a story to explain a trauma does not predict health improvements. Rather, the person must build or construct a story over the course of writing.

In our own research, it took years for me to appreciate the power of story construction. Oftentimes, someone would write about a traumatic experience and, on their first writing day, they could sew together a perfect story: a clear beginning, middle, and end; a seamless explanation why things had happened as they did. Often I would be transfixed by these stories because the author appeared so insightful and psychologically healthy. What bothered me, however, was that very few of these people showed any benefits from the writing. It's now clear that they had already constructed their stories. Perhaps they should have been writing about something else. Writing is beneficial only if you are trying to make sense of an event you don't understand.

The idea of constructing a story is similar to that of psychological growth. Expressive writing, like psychotherapy, or human relationships must exhibit change over time to be healthy. If you found yourself writing about the same trauma in the same way over the entire four-day writing exercise, it is not likely that writing about it was particularly beneficial for you.

Changing Perspectives

As a trauma or emotional upheaval unfolds, we tend to look at it exclusively from our own perspective. Only with time are we able to begin to appreciate what others were thinking, feeling, and seeing during the same period. Recent linguistic research is now finding that the ability to see an upheaval from different perspectives may be particularly beneficial (Campbell and Pennebaker 2003). The key to perspectives comes from an unlikely source: pronouns. Remember pronouns from high school? I, me, my, we, you, he, she, they, etc. It turns out that pronouns are extremely important in understanding how we write. For example, if you use a high number of first- person singular pronouns (I, me, my, mine, myself) you are emphasizing your personal perspective and you also may be self-focused. This is often good when writing about traumatic experiences. But the research indicates that it is healthy to write about other people, as well.

Go back to your four days of writing. You might even go through and circle all of the first-person singular pronouns. Are you using these pronouns at roughly the same rate from day to day in your writing? People tend to benefit more from emotional writing if their usage rates of the first-person singular change a great deal from one day to the next. In fact, if your rates are very similar from day to day, you are less likely to show health improvements.

Changes in pronoun use suggest changes in perspective. When dealing with something as massive as a trauma, it is important to try to see it from several different angles. It's not that any one perspective is any better or more valid than others. Instead, it's important just to get a sense of some of the many dimensions of the trauma you experienced.

Putting It All Together

You might think it peculiar that I'm telling you about the secrets of healthy writing in chapter 4. You may ask, "Why, didn't you mention these gems before the four-day writing exercise?" The answer is simple. If you knew that you should use a high number of positive emotion words and a moderate number of negative emotion words, if you had to construct a story, and bounce around in your use of pronouns, you would have been thinking about the words rather than your traumatic experience.

When looking back at your writing, you may have noticed that you naturally wrote in most of the ways that have been found to be healthy.

Unfortunately, some of the writing techniques probably require some practice for them to become more natural. That's why there are more chapters in this workbook.

In most ways, I hope that the four-day writing exercise was extremely beneficial for you. So much so that you don't feel like writing anymore, at least, not at this time in your life. If that *is* how you feel, then slowly put the book down, and walk quietly away. To be honest, that is exactly what I would do.

On the other hand, you may feel as though you would like to learn more about various writing strategies. Or maybe you are just a glutton for punishment. In either case, the following chapters have been put together as a series of writing exercises to help expand your horizon of expressive writing.

~ Part II ~

Experimenting with Writing

There is no absolute right way to disclose traumatic experiences. The four-day writing exercise in chapter 3 is the most rigorously tested method available. Although it works with a large percentage of people in reducing the unwanted effects of emotional upheavals, it is far from perfect. Think of the four-day writing technique as your basic no-frills, stripped-down floor model. Researchers are currently studying other writing strategies that, on occasion, have boosted the power of expressive writing. Some methods have been quite successful for some people, but not for others

In the following sections, several experimental methods are described. The exercises are not introduced in any systematic order. Rather, they represent a broad spectrum of potentially valuable ways of writing for you to experiment with on your own.

For most techniques, a brief ten-minute writing exercise is suggested. Other exercises are recommended to last only five minutes and others as long as twenty minutes. These relatively brief exercises are designed to give you a taste of a particular approach. If it helps, keep a clock beside you so that you write for the minimum recommended time. If you find that it is helpful or in some way satisfies your creative urges, expand your writing beyond the recommended minimum. In fact, you need not feel compelled to use a clock at all if you think it might constrict you. Also, you might try the same exercises several days in a row.

For each of the exercises, first read about them and see if they make sense to you. You are the expert. Try them out and discard those methods that don't work. You also can invent your own methods and styles of writing.

Chapter 5

Breaking Mental Blocks: Stream of Consciousness and Semiautomatic Writing

It's not uncommon for someone to plan on writing about an emotional event and then wind up staring at a blank piece of paper or a blank computer screen. You may know the feeling. You have a great deal to say but you don't know where to start. Or you may begin, but everything you write sounds false, stilted, or just plain stupid.

One reason people develop mental blocks about writing is that often they are too self-critical. The insistent voice of the censor in their head tells them that they need to write artistically or perfectly. That censor might be your high school English teacher, your parent, or someone you want to impress. To get expressive writing, you must dispense with the censor and give yourself permission to write anything, no matter how badly flawed you may think it is.

Stream of Consciousness Writing

One dependable method of writing is called "stream of consciousness" writing. The idea behind this type of writing is that you simply track your thoughts and feelings on paper as they occur. The only rule is that you must write continuously. Don't try to censor yourself. Before discussing it in any detail, try it out.

Exercise: Stream of Consciousness Writing

Beginning below, write in a stream of consciousness manner for ten minutes or until the two writing pages are filled. As you write, simply track your thoughts and feelings as they occur. Just write what you are thinking about, what you are feeling, hearing, smelling, or noticing. It is important for your writing simply to follow your stream of thought. Don't worry about spelling, grammar, or sentence structure. Remember that this writing is for you alone and that you can destroy it when you are finished. Just begin writing and don't stop.

William James, an early founder of modern psychology, was one of the first people to explore the concept of a stream of consciousness. His idea was that our stream of consciousness reveals a great deal about us. He made the following four general observations about it:

1. Every thought is ultimately personal. We know what it means but others may not. In a sense, then, every thought you write has some kind of meaning to you.

2. Thoughts are sensibly continuous (like a stream, thought 1 is related to thought 2 and thought 2 is related to thought 3; but thought 3 may not be related to thought 1). In other words, thoughts don't appear randomly, although they may appear as if they do. Look over your writing and explore your transitions. Why did one thought lead to the next one? What was the connection between them?

3. We can consciously think of only one thing at a time. Even though our brains may be detecting and analyzing sights, sounds, hunger pangs, and bittersweet memories of last night—all at the same time—at any given instant, we can be consciously aware of only one of these thoughts or perceptions.

4. It is meaningful to explore what we do think about, as well as what we actively don't think about. At some level, our mind chooses where our stream of thought goes. In your own writing, did you consciously choose to avoid a topic? Or subtly move your thinking (or typing) in a direction that it would not normally have gone?

Topical Stream of Consciousness Writing

Stream of consciousness writing can be used in many ways. If you are blocked about writing on a particular topic, you can focus your writing on that subject. This topic could be a particular emotional issue, a boring report for your job, or an important writing sample that others will evaluate ultimately. If you don't have any problems writing about something, you can skip this section. But if there is a particular issue or project that you simply can't start, this may help.

Topical stream of consciousness writing uses the same principles as the stream of consciousness writing that you used at the beginning of this chapter. The only difference is that, as you write, you should stay on the topic. Some possible prompts to get you going include the following:

~ I'm sitting here unable to write about _____. Why am I having trouble writing about this?

~ Thinking about this topic brings up a number of disconnected thoughts, including _____

~ In my life, there have been other times that I've been blocked about writing. How is this time similar? What is it about me that won't let me get started?

~ This topic is arousing a lot of emotions in me. Some of these emotions include _____

You can see the idea behind these prompts. Merely addressing the problem of writing is the first step in getting past a writing block. Indeed, several recent studies have suggested that simply labeling the problem and our feelings associated with it can help. Once we have a better understanding of the factors holding us back from writing, we can move forward.

Topical stream of consciousness writing sometimes can be thought of as a priming-the-pump method. Once you start writing about why you are having trouble writing about the topic, ideas about the topic start flowing. If this happens, go with it. You can always erase your stream of consciousness meanderings later (if this is for a report at work).

Exercise: Topical Stream of Consciousness Writing

As a simple exercise, why not try out the topical stream of consciousness writing? Here are the basic instructions: For the next ten minutes, write about that issue that you are having trouble writing about. Write continuously without worrying about spelling or grammar. You might start by using one of the prompts described above.

Semiautomatic Writing

If you are interested in the occult, most likely you've heard of automatic writing. The main idea behind semiautomatic writing is that it is possible to put yourself into a passive, almost trancelike, mental state and write at the same time. Some people report that their hands begin writing automatically. Frequently, this "automatic writing" is attributed to spirits, angels, demons, aliens, or some other paranormal phenomenon. However, a generation of psychological research has shown that these feelings of being possessed are simple illusions (Wegner 2002).

What is interesting about the automatic writing phenomenon is that it can be used as a way to turn off your mind's censor. If something is bothering you and you're not sure what it is, a form of automatic writing may be useful. Let's not call it automatic writing, however. How about semiautomatic writing? By the way, if you have been abducted by aliens, are a firm believer in demonic possession, or think that alien forces are controlling your mind, skip this section.

Exercise: Semiautomatic Writing.

Semiautomatic writing can work using a computer or writing by hand. The only rule is that you must not look at what you are writing. If you use a computer, simply turn off the monitor. For writing in longhand, get a cloth or towel and drape it over your writing hand and the paper. You can also simply shut your eyes or look in another direction. Before you begin writing, try to clear your mind. You might try focusing on your breathing, your emotions, or some object.

Once your attention is elsewhere, begin writing. Don't pay conscious attention to what you are writing. If you are typing, you will undoubtedly make errors. If writing by hand, you won't write within the lines. Don't worry about it. Just let yourself write without paying attention to the writing process itself. Try writing this way for a solid ten minutes.

When you finish, read what you have written. Sometimes it will be just a jumble of words and letters. But at other times you may find yourself addressing important issues. Keep in mind that there is no magic in this strategy. It is a way for you to touch on topics that you may not be aware of or that you may be avoiding. Indeed, some people have suggested that the results of semiautomatic writing are a little like dreams. They give us glimpses of the issues that are bothering us.

~ Chapter 6 ~

Appreciating the Good in a Sometimes Bad World

Traumatic experiences have the potential to touch every part of our lives in good and bad ways. After a tragedy, for example, people often report that they've come away with a stronger sense of their social connections and a redis-covered sense of meaning in their lives. Analysis of various writing samples con-sistently finds that those people who can express positive emotions while writing about tragic events tend to benefit most from expressive writing.

Let's be clear from the outset. If you've experienced a trauma, your friends may have told you a number of optimistic, stupid-sounding things like these:

"In a few years you will look back at this and laugh."
No, you probably won't.

"Look on the good side, at least [fill in ridiculous platitude here]."
There may not be a good side worth looking at now.

"Hey, cheer up!"
Hey, buzz off!

After you've experienced a trauma, other people often want you to be happy because your pain is difficult for them to deal with. If you could put on a cheerful, upbeat face, they would be more comfortable. But, clearly, such false happiness is not true positive emotion. In this chapter, you will find a number of exercises that may be helpful in encouraging you to draw on some of your deeper reservoirs of love, meaning, and contentment. No false grins or cheerful-ness are expected (or wanted).

Acknowledging and Expressing Positive Emotion

In the late 1980s, two psychologists, Camille Wortman and Roxanne Silver (1989), published a highly controversial article entitled "Myths of Coping with Loss." Drawing on a large number of academically sound studies, the authors pointed out that after the death of a spouse or child, not everyone gets depressed. In fact, almost half of those who have experienced a major loss are healthy and happy soon afterward—often within a month. One reason people were shocked by these findings was because it is not socially acceptable to be happy and well-adjusted in the face of an overwhelming personal trauma.

As discussed in chapter 4, the ability to use words that convey positive emotions when writing about a traumatic experience predicts better health after the writing exercise. Some of the hundreds of positive emotion words include the following:

love	joy	happy	caring	pretty
nice	peace	good	laughter	strong
dignity	trust	courageous	accepting	calm
fun	gentle	humor	inspiring	kiss
perfect	proud	contented	secure	satisfied
glad	merry	romantic	thankful	easy

For some people, using positive emotion words when writing about trauma requires practice. In the space below, try writing about a negative experience for ten minutes using as many positive emotion words as possible. You can use as many negative emotion words you need, as well. All the time, try to be honest about the experience. In other words, don't lie to yourself that something was joyful when it wasn't.

When selecting a negative event, start off with something only slightly negative. Don't jump into a massive trauma. The goal here is to practice using both positive emotion words and, when needed, negative emotion words. In fact, if you can use, say, "not calm" instead of "worried," you will have used one of the positive emotion words. (Research suggests that using "not happy" is better for your health than "sad.")

Exercise: Using Positive Emotion Words

So, here we go. For the next ten minutes, write continuously about a negative experience that happened to you. Describe what happened, how you felt then and now, and anything else that seems relevant. Try to use as many positive emotions words as you can while, at the same time, staying true to the experience. Write continuously without stopping.

---

romantic thankful easy love joy happy caring pretty nice peace good laughter strong dignity trust courageous

(word-grid activity page — terms arranged along all four edges: merry, glad, satisfied, secure, contented, proud, perfect, kiss, inspiring, humor, gentle, fun, calm, accepting, courageous, trust, dignity, strong; and repeated lists of appreciation words around the margins)

romantic thankful easy love joy happy caring pretty nice peace good laughter strong dignity trust courageous accepting calm fun gentle humor inspiring kiss perfect proud contented secure satisfied glad merry romantic thankful easy love joy

If my calculations are correct, the last ten minutes of writing were more difficult than you had thought they would be. Read back over what you just wrote and see where you used positive as opposed to negative emotion words. Where were you honest with yourself and where were you not? In retrospect, how could you have used more positive emotion words in describing the event and its aftermath?

Exercise: Finding Occasional Positive Feelings

Let's try this exercise one more time. This time, don't look at the positive emotion word list. Write about the same experience for ten minutes and think about where the occasional positive feeling might bubble up.

Now that you have completed both writing exercises, take a few minutes to reflect on how you felt after completing each one. Most people feel far more comfortable and satisfied after finishing the second exercise compared with the first. Start to pay attention to the words you use when talking or writing about upheavals in your life. Acknowledge and express positive feelings when you can.

Benefit-Finding

Another approach for recognizing positive emotions is to actively look for the benefits that may have resulted from a trauma or emotional upheaval. Several research teams have found that people who are able to find meaning or other benefits in misfortune cope much better with their traumas than people who can find no benefit at all in their misfortunes (King and Miner 2000). Also there have been some studies on expressive writing where people were explicitly requested to write about their traumas in a way that emphasized their positive experiences. For many people, this benefit-finding writing perspective was beneficial.

Exercise: Finding Benefits in Upheavals

For this next exercise, try your hand at benefit-finding. Think of an emotional upheaval or another negative experience in your past. For the next ten minutes, briefly describe the event and then tell about any benefits that came from it. Such benefits could include a greater understanding of yourself and others, a change in the direction of your life that may have avoided more heartache or led to greater happiness or growth. When writing, be honest and open with yourself.

Broaching Forgiveness

"Forgive and forget." There is more than a kernel of truth to this adage. Being able to say "I forgive you" or, if you are the wrongdoer, "Please forgive me," can be a significant step in the healing process. Nevertheless, asking for or granting forgiveness often is not possible. Perhaps the other person is not available or does not want to deal with you. Other times, merely talking to another person about your upsetting experience will only open old wounds that can't be healed. Especially when there are social barriers to forgiveness, writing about past injustice can be helpful.

Granting Forgiveness When You're the Victim

For many people, forgiving others for upending their lives can be an almost-impossible task. To forgive the perpetrator of a terrible act implies letting the perpetrator get away with an injustice. Not forgiving, however, can result in the continuation of feelings of anger and bitterness. And, although we rarely admit it, truly resenting or hating another person can be satisfying. Forgiveness, then, is potentially disrupting. The payoff, however, is that it can increase the odds that you will be able to get on with your life.

Exercise: Granting Forgiveness

This is a writing exercise for you if you have suffered an injustice as a result of another person's behavior and you feel as though you could forgive that person. Although this exercise is designed to last only ten minutes, if you have a serious forgiveness issue to deal with, consider writing for twenty minutes per day for three to four consecutive days.

Before writing, think about a specific situation where you were treated badly by another person. Recall how you felt before, during, and after the event. More importantly, imagine how that person might have felt. Why do you think he or she felt that way? Don't demonize the other person. She or he is a human being just as you are, with fears, insecurities, and stories of their own.

For the next ten minutes, write about your deepest emotions and thoughts concerning this event in your life. Briefly mention what led up to the event. Focus more on the other person (or people) who were responsible for what happened. What do you think was going on in their life at the time? How do you think they felt afterward? What will it take for you to forgive their actions? If you feel as though you can forgive them, do so on paper. Explore what being able to forgive them means to you and to them. As always, write continuously and write in an uncensored manner. Make a plan that no one else will see your writing.

Asking for Forgiveness When You Have Caused Suffering

Just as we have all been victims at some points in our lives, we also have caused suffering in others, either intentionally or accidentally. Although asking forgiveness via expressive writing is a socially isolated act, it can be of great value psychologically. More than anything else, it forces writers to acknowledge their own part in causing another's unhappiness.

Exercise: Asking for Forgiveness

Before writing, spend some time thinking about something you've done in the past that caused someone else emotional pain. Think carefully of what led up to the event, what was going on in your mind at the time, and how you felt afterward. Imagine how the other person felt and what he or she may have thought. Consider also how your action may have indirectly affected the other person's family or friends. Finally, think how you might have felt and behaved if the same event had happened to you.

As with the granting-forgiveness exercise, use the following writing task as an experiment. If you have an issue that is central to who you are, then consider writing for twenty minutes a day for three to four consecutive days with the same general instructions. In addition, you may have more than one person to whom you would like to say "I'm sorry." Try the ten-minute asking-for-forgiveness exercise for those people who are the most relevant to your life.

For the next ten minutes, briefly describe what happened and what role you played in causing pain for another person. Don't use your writing to justify your actions. Rather, focus on the other person's feelings and thoughts. If you can, express your sorrow for this event. You might write out an apology to the other person as if they were going to read it. You should also explore the possibility of what it would take to make amends with this person and/or their friends and family now. As always, write continuously and write in an uncensored manner. Plan that no one else will see your writing.

~ Chapter 7 ~

Constructing and Editing Your Story

Research dealing with expressive writing suggests that people are most likely to benefit from writing about a trauma if they can build a coherent story of their experience. The operative word here is *building* a story—not just having one. Unfortunately, it isn't always clear what makes a good story. What may be a good story for one person may seem superficial or deluded to another.

Despite the many disagreements about what constitutes a coherent story, most people agree on some of the basic elements. Whether you are writing a novel or about a personal trauma, the following features are generally included:

A DESCRIPTION OF THE SETTING. When and where did the event occur? What was going on at the time?

A SENSE OF THE MAIN CHARACTERS. Who was involved and what were they doing? What were they thinking and feeling? What were you doing, thinking, and feeling before the event?

A CLEAR DESCRIPTION OF THE EVENT OR UPHEAVAL. What triggered it and what happened? How did you react as it was unfolding?

THE IMMEDIATE AND LONG-TERM CONSEQUENCES. What happened as a result of the event? How did this upheaval influence your life and the lives of others? How did the event shape your current situation and emotional state?

THE MEANING OF THE STORY. Why are you telling this story to yourself or others? Why has it had such an effect on you? What have you learned as a result of your experience?

Not all good stories include all of these features. In fact, some of the best and most helpful narratives to evolve from the expressive writing research started off with glaring holes. When they began writing, participants often didn't know exactly what had happened, what the real consequences were, or what any of it meant. However, over the several days of writing, they began to build a more coherent and meaningful story; one that made sense to them.

A Simple Story Construction Exercise

To illustrate the steps in constructing a meaningful story, this exercise is a two-step process. Rather than write about a massive upheaval in your life, think about some upsetting or confusing event that happened to you recently. Maybe it was a fight with a family member or friend; perhaps you had an unexpected conflict at work. Ideally, it should be something you've thought about a few times in the last couple of days. Do you have an event in mind? Good.

Exercise: Step 1—Just Write

Without thinking or censoring your thoughts, write for no more than ten minutes about what happened. Just let it out on paper. Don't try to impose any kind of structure on the event. No need to analyze it. Just write.

When you've finished, go back and read what you wrote. In all likelihood, your writing was much less random than you had thought it was. You probably put things together in a surprisingly organized way. As you read it, however, you will probably notice that you left some important things out and did not deal with some of the thoughts and emotions you may have.

Before proceeding to the next step, give yourself some time—perhaps a few minutes—to reconsider this event. When you return, your goal will be to write about the same event but with the idea of imposing more structure on it. That is, you will be asked to include information on the setting, the characters, the event itself, the consequences, and the meaning of the event, as though you were telling the story to someone else. Think about these instructions for a few minutes.

Exercise: Step 2—Constructing a Story

The reasons that humans in all cultures around the world tell stories is to convey complex ideas and emotions to others in organized and simple ways. The event you wrote about in Step 1 was probably moderately complex. If you were concerned with detail, you probably could have stretched the event to five or ten pages, maybe even to the size of a novel. We also create stories because they allow us to summarize complex events into smaller packages.

Consider the elements of a good coherent story. Focus especially on the event, its consequences, and its meaning. For this phase of the exercise, rewrite the event that you addressed in Step 1. This time, however, imagine that you are telling the story of the event to a stranger whom you will never see again. Be a good and honest storyteller. Once you begin writing, do not look at your original writing sample. Try to write your story in ten minutes but take more time if you need it.

When you have completed Step 2, go back and compare your two stories. How did they change? How do you feel about the event itself now that you have addressed it twice. Most people find the second writing less exciting to write about, but somehow it gets them past the event better. The second writing experience tends to force structure onto the upsetting event that was previously lacking. In fact, by now, you might consider the entire episode a bit tedious. Maybe you have a sense of wanting to move on to some other issues in your life. That is precisely the point of writing about the event two times.

Rewriting and Editing Your Traumatic Experience

The point of the simple story construction exercises was to stimulate your thinking about the idea that personal traumas are a form of story. If you are able to transform a chaotic personal upheaval into an honest and coherent story, you are more likely to be able to get on with your life and move past the event.

Just as you can use the story construction process on relatively minor upheavals, you can use it for dealing with major traumas as well. There are some important differences however. A major personal trauma can be a story in itself. It also can loom so large in your life that it can create multiple mini-stories. A trauma, then, has the potential to grow into a novel where one event cascades into others; each one with its own plot and meaning.

To apply the story construction process to your own major upset or trauma, it is first necessary for you to write about it using the instructions detailed in chapter 3. From a research perspective, the chapter 3 expressive writing method has consistently produced the most promising results. Once you have completed the chapter 3 writing, you can use that experience as the base for the following exercises. Two overlapping techniques are outlined. The first encourages you to reconsider your trauma as a true story, using all of the elements a story uses. The second technique suggests ways to go back and edit your trauma narrative. In both cases, you can write in the limited space of this workbook. However, you are urged to attempt this broad rewriting and editing in your own notebook since it may take much more space than is available here.

Working Your Trauma into a Story

If you kept your writing from chapter 3, go back and read it. If you did not keep it, try to reconstruct what you wrote. It is likely that you dealt with several issues in your writing that actually may have been more than one emotional upheaval. For the purpose of this exercise, try to focus on what you believe to be the most central event or issue for you.

Reread and think about the essential aspects of your expressive writing. In your original writing, it is likely that you found yourself dealing with tangential issues, or even discussing topics that distracted you from what you really needed to write about. As you read and think about this topic, consider how you can begin to make this experience an organized and meaningful story. As always, this story is for you and you alone, which means it must be honest in every way.

For this exercise, you should write for twenty minutes on a single occasion. You may find, however, that a single writing session for this task is impossible. If you need to write more, then do it. Each person's story is very different. Some people can reduce their trauma story to a simple theme and tie up the main points in ten minutes. Others will write for several days. Either way works, but try to write for about twenty minutes at a time.

Before you begin writing, review the essential elements of a good story: setting, characters, a description of the event and its immediate and long-term consequences. Most important, focus on the meaning of the event. Also, it wouldn't hurt to consider the lessons of chapter 5. That is, emphasizing the positive or potential benefits of an unwanted experience may yield better health.

Exercise: Basic Instructions for Writing Your Story

For the next twenty minutes, work your traumatic experience into a story with a clear beginning, middle, and end. Describe the experience and how it affected you and others. What is the meaning of this event for you? In your writing, express your emotions freely and be honest with yourself. Once you begin writing, write continuously for the entire twenty minutes. If your story goes in a direction you didn't anticipate, follow your heart. You can always write again tomorrow.

As always, this writing is for you alone. Don't worry about spelling, grammar, or sentence structure.

It is not uncommon for people to find it difficult to make a coherent story about their overwhelming traumas, especially on their first try. If this was your experience, consider writing about the same event again. Each time you write, however, try to change your orientation and thinking. Work to make the event more organized and structured. If you feel it is warranted, write the story over and over until you become bored with it. Getting bored with your own trauma, by the way, is a sign of progress. It is a signal from your brain telling you to get on with your life.

The Possible Power of Editing and Reworking Your Writing

We now come to a debatable topic. Several people I deeply respect believe that editing and rewriting your expressive writing is both a powerful tool and a healthy activity. Other people just don't like to edit or rewrite. This is clearly an issue of personal taste.

When writing about a trauma, it is often impossible to know what features of the story are most important. Sometimes you think one aspect may have changed your life but, on further reflection, you may realize that something else was far more significant. When you go back and edit your expressive writings, you can remake your own history with the benefit of hindsight. This is not to say you are reinventing your trauma. Rather, extensive editing and rewriting of your story can help you to focus on what is most relevant to your life right now.

If you have been doing most of the writing exercises in this workbook, you have several possible writing samples to work with. Perhaps the most relevant is either the expressive writing exercise in chapter 3 or the trauma-into-a-story exercise you just completed. You can use either, but for the purpose of this next exercise let's use your trauma-into-a-story exercise.

Exercise: Rewriting and Editing Your Story

The purpose of this exercise is to rewrite your personal writing sample into a more organized, honest, and coherent story. Unlike every other writing exercise, this time you should collaborate with your mind's "censor." That is, you should look at the logical flow of your writing, your writing style, and what you intended to say. Your goal is to make this a better story in every way.

As a first step, make a neat copy of the story, perhaps copy it onto a computer or into a notebook. Correct any spellings or awkward sentences. Be honest with yourself in reporting on the feelings and thoughts you had while writing it. Then, gradually work on the structure of your story. You may have to work on it sentence by sentence. Does each idea flow in a meaningful and logical way?

After you have worked on it for a while, take some time away from it. Take a break for several minutes, hours, or even days. When you return, read it again and make more changes. This story is for you and it should express your deepest emotions and thoughts in an open and honest way. It should also be a story with a clear beginning, middle, and end. Above all, it should have a point to it. Why are you telling this story? What benefits has this experience brought to you?

If it looks as if this editing process will take a long time, give yourself a deadline by which to complete it. If you find that you are becoming obsessed with this project, stop. The purpose of this writing exercise is for you to work through the trauma; not to wrap yourself into it. If you can't seem to find any meaning in the event no matter how hard you look, then simply admit that fact and walk away. There are some experiences in life that may not have any meaning or value to them.

As a final note, people vary tremendously in what they consider to be satisfying and meaningful stories. Trust your own instincts in your writing. If, after writing something, you feel as though you have gained some benefit from it, even though other people might see it as a jumbled mess, then pat yourself on your back. You have succeeded.

~ Chapter 8 ~

Changing Perspectives

Some of the most exciting recent discoveries in expressive writing have to do with the role of perspective. People who benefit the most from writing about their traumas change the ways in which they focus on the trauma from day to day. For example, on one day they may focus primarily on their own feelings and experiences; on other days they might talk about the thoughts and feelings of others who were involved in the trauma.

Because the work on changing one's perspective is very new, it is hard to understand why it is related to improved health. One possibility may be that if you can look at an upsetting event from different angles, you are better able to stand back from it. In other words, the ability to adopt alternative perspectives both requires and reflects a certain detachment from the subject you are thinking about.

There have been some preliminary studies where people were asked to try to change their perspectives while writing about personal upheavals. The initial results are promising, although some people clearly enjoy switching their perspective more than others. Two perspective-changing exercises are described in this chapter. Try them out for yourself to see whether you find them valuable.

Writing in the Third Person

Many novelists struggle with which voice to present their main character. What are the implications if the story begins using the first person as opposed to a third person perspective? Consider the first two sentences of the following trauma essay:

FIRST-PERSON VOICE. When I was seventeen, my father left home. I was trapped in an emotional war between my sister and mother. They hated each other and tried to pull me into their battles. Even writing about it brings up the pain and sadness I always felt in our house.

THIRD-PERSON VOICE. When he was seventeen, his father left home. He was trapped in an emotional war between his sister and mother. The two hated each other and tried to pull him into their battles. Even writing about it brings up the pain and sadness he always felt in their house.

Changing the perspective from the first person (I, me, our) to the third person (he, she, him, her, they) subtly alters the tone of the story. The third-person view is more distanced and, from the reader's viewpoint, safer. It is not uncommon for people who have lived through a truly horrific trauma (such as torture) to initially describe the experience in the third person. Only when they begin to feel more comfortable talking about it will they begin speaking in the first person.

Two third-person writing exercises are suggested below. The first is to practice with writing about a recent problem or conflict. Once you feel comfortable using third person, try the second exercise in which you write about an aspect of the trauma or emotional upheaval most relevant to your life.

Brief Perspective-Switching Exercises

Think of an event, conflict, or other issue that you have been dealing with lately. This should not be a huge trauma, rather, it should be an event that you think of as an annoyance. As detailed below, your goal is to write about this experience twice, each time for about ten minutes. Give yourself a break of at least several minutes between the two writing exercises.

Exercise: Writing in the First Person

For the next ten minutes, write about your emotions and thoughts concerning a recent annoying event that you have been thinking or worrying about. Describe matters from your normal first-person perspective. In your writing, describe the event and your reactions to it. You may link it to other events from your past or present. Once you begin, write continuously the entire ten minutes.

Exercise: Writing in the Third Person

Before beginning to write this exercise, look back and read over what you wrote as part of the first-person exercise. For the next ten minutes, write about the same general issue, but this time use the third-person voice. If you are female, replace your normal "I" with "she" (or "he" if you are a male). In other words, write about the actions and emotions of the main character (who is you) as though you were observing everything from a third-person perspective. Try to include the same basic information that you included when you were writing in the first person.

On completing the third-person exercise, stand back and evaluate how writing in this voice felt compared with your normal first-person writing. Many people report that they have mixed feelings when they first try it. They say, "It just doesn't feel natural." This is an issue of practice. The more you use the third person in your writing, the more comfortable it will feel.

Before giving up on the third-person approach, try this exercise again at a later time by writing on another topic. Instead of starting with first person and then switching to the third person, do it in the reverse order. That is, first describe the event from the distanced third-person voice and then write about it a second time in the first person.

Addressing Your Trauma from the Third-Person Perspective

The brief perspective-switching exercise was really a way of practicing third-person writing. The true potential value of the third-person voice becomes evident when dealing with particularly powerful emotional upheavals. If you continue to be haunted by a trauma or an emotional upheaval, you may find that writing from the third-person perspective is beneficial. As with all the exercises in this book, you need to try it out to see if it will work for you.

Exercise: Writing as a Third-Person Observer

For this next exercise, it is recommended that you write about a powerful emotional experience that continues to dominate your thoughts and feelings. In your writing, try to let go and explore your deepest emotions and thoughts. Instead of referring to this trauma as "my experience" or "my feelings," write entirely in the third person, as if you were reporting on your own experience as the observer of a major trauma that happened to someone else. What happened to this person? What led up to the event? How did the person react and why? How were other people affected? How does the person to whom this event happened feel now? What meaning can you draw from this person's experience?

Write continuously for an entire twenty-minute session and maintain the third-person perspective. If you slip into the first-person, strike it out and change what you wrote to the third person. Remember that this writing is for you alone.

REFLECTING ON THIRD PERSON. Occasionally, the use of the third person can be a powerful tool for dealing with highly charged emotional events. Oftentimes, those emotions and experiences that are the rawest and most painful can be dealt with best by using a more detached voice. With repeated telling, you can begin to move to the more natural first-person voice. This exercise should be viewed as a first step. If it is helpful, try using the third person for other assignments. The ability to use both first- and third-person perspectives can help you maintain emotional flexibility when dealing with any emotional upsets that may come your way.

Writing Flexibly with Pronouns

Pronouns? Who would ever have thought that you would be reading a book that extolled the virtues of pronouns—or any part of speech for that matter? Nevertheless, as noted in chapter 4, pronouns may be critically important for understanding the power of expressive writing. This was an accidental discovery. Researchers who were studying writing samples from old experiments found that those experiment participants who changed in the ways they used pronouns from one writing day to the next had better health in subsequent months. Those who used pronouns in the same ways day after day demonstrated only minor improvements in their health (Campbell and Pennebaker 2003).

A closer look indicates that the central distinction occurs between the word "I" and all other pronouns (you, they, me, we, etc). If the person uses the word "I" a great deal on one day and other pronouns on the next day, that's good. Similarly, using other pronouns on one day (but not much of "I") and then a great deal of "I" on the next day is also good. Using the same pronouns in the same way across all the days of expressive writing is associated with minimal health improvements following the writing intervention.

These may be extremely important results. Of course, pronouns themselves don't make people healthy or sick. Instead, they reflect how people think about their traumatic experiences. If people write about specific traumas for several days in a row and always use the same pronouns, their thinking is probably rather rigid. Maybe they re-examine their own perspective every day; maybe they focus only on someone else's perspective. The writers who benefit the most, however, clearly flip their perspectives on a day-by-day basis. One day, the writer might describe another's actions and emotions; the next day he or she might focus on their own actions and feelings.

It's tempting to set up a writing exercise where you are asked to use pronouns from List A on the first day of writing and pronouns from List B on the next day. Unfortunately, it won't work. Past experience with this shows that people can spend so much time looking at the word lists while trying to use the right pronouns that they forget what they are writing about. A better approach is to think about perspectives. Focusing on different people, including yourself, from essay to essay may cause the pronouns to follow.

Virtually all personal upheavals are social. A traumatic event may happen just to you, but almost always it also affects others, either directly or indirectly. In all likelihood, another person was involved in the unfolding of your trauma. When writing about traumas, the reason we use pronouns at such high rates is because we need to talk about both "me" and the other people.

In the next writing exercise, try describing an emotionally important event from several perspectives. Plan for this exercise to last about twenty minutes, devoting five minutes to each of four perspectives. In the first five-minute period, lay out what happened, who was involved, and what is happening now. The second five-minute period should focus exclusively on your perspective, feelings, and actions. The third five-minute writing period should deal with one or more other people in this story. In the fourth and final five-minute writing period you should stand back and try to integrate all of the perspectives that you developed earlier in this exercise. For these exercises, move from one writing instruction to the next without stopping.

Exercise: Perspective 1—the Big Picture

For the next five minutes, write continuously about an emotional upheaval that is important to your life. In your writing, describe what happened and who was involved. How did you and others react to this event and how is it affecting all of you now? As soon as you are finished with this section, continue with the exercise for Perspective 2.

Exercise: Perspective 2—I, Me, and My

For the next five minutes, write about the same emotional upheaval but focus exclusively on your perspective. What did *you* think, feel, and do? How have *your* behaviors affected others? What would *you* like others to know about *your* situation? Write continuously and honestly. When you are finished, continue to Perspective 3.

Exercise: Perspective 3—The Other People

Now, you are halfway finished with these exercises. For the next five minutes write about the same general trauma but focus on the role of another person or group of people. What was and is going on in their minds? What did they do and feel? What do you think they would like others to know about their perspective? Try to look into their hearts and assume that they are at least as complicated as you are. Write continuously and when finished move onto Perspective 4.

Exercise: Perspective 4—Another Big Picture

Before you begin writing, look back at what you have written so far. Have you been honest with yourself and about the other people? For this last five-minute writing period, again tell the story of this trauma. Take a broad perspective in terms of what happened. What value or meaning can you and others draw from this experience? Write continuously the entire time.

The point of the last exercise was to motivate you to think about adopting multiple perspectives when dealing with a complex emotional event. Go back and examine your use of pronouns from perspective to perspective. Ideally, you changed a great deal in the percentage of "I" words that you used. If the number of "I" words was similar across all four exercises, ask yourself why this was the case. It might be beneficial to try this assignment again and consciously try to change your pronoun usage to force a change in perspective.

If you found this exercise helpful, consider writing about other emotional upheavals in your life. For each experience, try to write about it on several occasions, adopting a slightly different perspective each time. As you become adept at viewing the same upheaval from different directions, you will also find yourself becoming more and more detached from the event.

~ Chapter 9 ~

Experimenting with Context

When and where people write may influence what they write. Some situations can make us defensive while others allow us to be vulnerable. Although very little solid research has been conducted on writing context, a smattering of findings suggest that changes in the time and place of writing can affect people's orientation to an emotional upheaval. This chapter requires you to conduct your own small experiments. Although some places, potential audiences, and times will be suggested, you will need to draw on your own experiences to devise the best contexts for your writing.

In reading this chapter follow your instincts. Be playful and scientific at the same time. As always, embrace what works and discard what doesn't.

Locations and Settings

Where you are affects how you think. If you walk by a restaurant, you often can't help but think of food. The kind of music you hear in a grocery story can influence what you buy. A recent study, for example, found that if people heard Italian music in a wine shop, they were more likely to buy Italian wine (North, Hargreaves, and McKendrick 1997). It follows, then, that where you write can subtly affect the memories and emotions that may bubble to the surface.

Writing settings can vary along an infinite number of dimensions. Rather than propose a list of places to write, four relatively simple contexts for writing will be suggested. Try them and see what happens.

Writing to Boost Self-Focus—Mirrors

Whenever we see our reflections or hear our own voices, we automatically become more self-attentive. Beginning in the 1970s, an extraordinary number of experiments found that when people were put in front of a mirror they became more honest and aware of who they were. Although the effects were striking, they were subtle. People didn't have any idea that the mirrors were affecting them (Wicklund 1979). Is it possible that writing in the presence of a mirror can influence writing? In a recent test of this idea, we found that for some people, writing in front of a mirror was a particularly powerful experience. Try it out.

Exercise: Writing in Front of a Mirror

Whether you are writing by hand or on a laptop computer, find a place where there is a reasonably large mirror. The best setting would be writing in front of a mirror that reflects your face or, better yet, your entire body. If you are writing on a stationary computer, bring a mirror beside you, even if it is a hand-held mirror. Your general writing assignment will be to explore an emotionally important issue in your life and how it is related to who you are.

WRITING INSTRUCTIONS. Look at yourself in the mirror. Gaze into your own eyes; look at your face. See yourself as others see you and as you see yourself. While looking at your image, think about a significant personal issue and how it relates to where you are in your life, your connections to others, and who you really are. After closely examining yourself in the mirror for several minutes, begin writing.

Write continuously for a minimum of ten minutes. Every now and then, look back at your reflection. Be honest with yourself.

When you have finished this assignment, review what you have written. Did you find this a valuable exercise? If so, try writing about other significant emotional experiences in this way as well.

FINDING A SAFE AND PEACEFUL CONTEXT. People are often able to disclose extremely personal stories when they feel most secure. Confessing to another person or through prayer in a house of worship, conversing with a close friend under the summer stars, or even confiding in a therapist's office are examples of places where we are able to let down our defenses. For this exercise, your goal is to find a setting where you normally feel safe to reveal yourself. Ideally, it should be a place where you generally don't write and is away from reminders of your everyday life.

Exercise: Finding a Safe Place to Write

Take this workbook or other notebook to a location where you feel particularly secure. It could be outdoors at a park or in the woods, in an unused classroom, a church or library, an old friend's house, or even a bench inside a shopping area or coffee shop. Before you begin writing, you must relax and appreciate your environment. Draw on the feelings of familiarity and connections with your past and with other people. If you have chosen a spiritual setting, consider offering a silent prayer.

WRITING INSTRUCTIONS. Write for at least ten minutes about an important experience in your past. Before writing, however, focus on your feelings of security and peace linked to the place you are in. Think about how this past experience connects with who you are now. In your writing, explore your emotions and thoughts about this past experience. Write continuously without censoring yourself.

At first, it sometimes can be difficult to adjust to a new situation when writing. If this experience was valuable, then return to this setting and address deeper, more significant issues. Even if this was not a particularly helpful exercise, consider trying other novel environments. You might look specifically for environments that touch on different parts of your past: spiritual, home, early childhood, school, or those unique places that only you might associate with safety, honesty, and trust.

USING SYMBOLS OF THE PAST. People using this workbook have experienced vastly different types of traumatic experiences. For some, this exercise may be inappropriate or too painful. For others, it may be ideally suited to confronting the past. Drawing on the Flip-Out Rule, use your own judgment about whether it could be helpful for you.

Growing scientific evidence suggests that many people who experienced traumas in their past can benefit from re-exposing themselves to some of the painful memories of the event. This technique, variously called *flooding, exposure therapy*, or *implosive therapy*, has been used to treat rape victims and other victims of violent abuse, as well as treating those suffering from crippling fears resulting from a large array of traumatic incidents (Foa and Kozak 1986). If your symptoms after a trauma are particularly troublesome, it is recommended that you seek the help of a psychotherapist. However, if you feel that you can benefit from a diluted form of exposure therapy, then try the following writing exercise.

Exercise: Remembering the Trauma

For this twenty-minute exercise, you will be writing about an emotional upheaval in your life associated with a particular place, person, even smell. You should choose a location for your writing that, typically, you don't use to write, perhaps a garage, a library, even a bathroom. Your task is to bring certain reminders or symbols of the trauma together in the place in which you will write. These reminders could be pictures, letters, clothing, almost anything that you associate with the upheaval. Once these symbols have all been assembled, follow the writing instructions.

WRITING INSTRUCTIONS. Before you begin writing, spend several minutes looking at, feeling, and even smelling the various symbols that you have collected. Let yourself experience some of the sensations and emotions of the past. (*Caution:* If you get too upset doing this, then stop, go to the store and get some ice cream instead.) After a few minutes, begin writing.

During the twenty minutes that you will be writing, explore your thoughts and feelings about this emotional upheaval in your life. How has it affected you in the past and how does it continue to influence you now? Briefly mention each of the symbols and explain why they are so powerful for you. You might tie this emotional experience to other aspects of your life, to your relationships, career, and family.

As always, write continuously and remember that this writing is for you and you alone. Also, remember the Flip-Out Rule: if you get too upset by your writing, simply stop.

Many people find this exercise extremely powerful. Often, the mere ability to verbalize one's fears and experiences can help to reduce their influence. Similarly, linking emotional experiences to important symbols of the past can help clarify the meaning of a terrible experience.

If you found this exercise valuable, it is advisable to try it again. The more times you do it, however, the more important it is to draw on other features of this workbook. That is, try to use positive emotion words, construct a story, and change perspective each time you write.

Exercise: Writing for Symbolic Audiences

The idea of a setting or context usually provokes thoughts of locations. Contexts are also defined by the people inhabiting them. If you are in an empty classroom, the thought of a teacher is often inescapable. Your childhood home probably evokes memories of many other people. These "invisible" other people, then, are part of the context.

Once we begin thinking of people as part of a setting, we can't escape thinking about how the implied presence of others might affect our thoughts, emotions, and how we write. Throughout this workbook, most writing assignments have been explicit in getting you to write to yourself rather than to another person. Many scholars have questioned whether this is even possible. While writing, you may have caught yourself thinking, "What will my friends (or spouse, child, enemy) think when they read this?" The reality is that we change our writing depending on who we think our audience might be.

In this exercise, you are asked to write about an important personal experience addressing different symbolic audiences. Although you will be asked to imagine that these other people will see your writing, don't show it to them. This writing exercise is for your eyes only.

WRITING INSTRUCTIONS. This exercise should take about twenty minutes. Your goal is to write about the same general experience for four completely different audiences. Plan to write about five minutes for each audience. Your writing topic should be something that is emotionally important to you. It could be something that happened to you years ago or more recently. Ideally, it should be something that involved another person who is or was close to you. Whether or not that person is alive is not important. Once you begin writing, don't stop until the five minutes are up. For each scenario, try to be as honest as possible.

AUDIENCE 1—AUTHORITY FIGURE: Imagine you must tell an authority figure in your life about this emotional experience. This authority figure must not be a part of the story you will be telling. The person could be a judge, boss, FBI agent, parent, or teacher. It should be someone with whom you've had a fairly formal relationship with, or someone you respect and fear slightly. Imagine that your writing will be evaluated by this authority figure.

In your writing, tell the authority figure about this important emotional experience in your life. What were your thoughts and feelings then and now and how has this experience affected your life since?

AUDIENCE 2—A CLOSE AND COMPASSIONATE FRIEND: Write about the same experience, but this time imagine that you will show your writing to a close friend. This friend should be someone you deeply trust and who will accept you no matter what you say. Also, this friend should not be linked to the experience in any direct way. If you can't think of such a friend, invent one.

In your writing, tell your friend about this important emotional experience in your life. What were your thoughts and feelings then and now and how has this experience affected your life since?

AUDIENCE 3—ANOTHER PERSON INVOLVED IN THIS EXPERIENCE:
For this five-minute writing exercise, imagine that your writing will be evaluated by someone directly related to this experience. Ideally, this should be someone with a very different perspective about what happened and its meaning.

In your writing, tell this person about this important emotional experience in your life. What were your thoughts and feelings then and now, and how has this experience affected your life since?

AUDIENCE 4—YOURSELF: For the final five-minute task, you should be the only audience. You are writing for yourself and no one else. If it would make the experience more powerful, look at yourself in a mirror before you start writing. Remember that you will destroy this writing sample as soon as you are finished.

In your writing, tell yourself about this important emotional experience in your life. What were your thoughts and feelings then and now and how has this experience affected your life since?

Now that you have completed all four writing tasks, go back and analyze how they differed from each other. Did you notice feeling different as you were writing each one? Did you feel that some were more genuine than others? Did any one task give you a different perspective on your experience?

This kind of writing assignment can be effective for getting you to appreciate the roles that other people have in your personal stories. It can be beneficial to write about an experience to more than one imagined audience. If you find that your story changes a great deal from audience to audience, you probably don't have a good understanding of it just yet. As with the perspective-changing exercises, writing to different audiences can help to give you a greater sense of detachment about the experience.

Playing with Writing Times

Some people work best in the early morning and others late at night. When you write is a matter of personal preference. As noted earlier, the only recommendation about when to write is that you should ensure that you have some free time after writing. The free time could be spent doing things like walking, driving, gardening, or washing dishes. Watching TV is a bad idea (it naturally blocks our ability to be self-reflective). After important writing sessions, it is essential that you have some time to continue thinking about your writing topic.

You may already have established the best times for you to write. Nevertheless, it never hurts to shake up your schedule a bit. Experiment with some of the writing exercises in this workbook at different times of the day. Some possibilities include the following:

~ **Early morning writing.** As soon as you wake up in the morning, begin writing. You can write in bed or some other place in your home. Decide what your topic will be before you go to bed. Feel free to change the topic based on how you feel that morning. Also, draw on any dreams you might have had that evening.

~ **Lunchtime writing.** Most of the exercises in this workbook take ten to twenty minutes. Even at work, you may be able to find that much time to do some serious writing during your lunch break. Ideally, your writing should start as soon as your break begins. This will allow you some free time after writing to think about it. You can even do this instead of eating a large lunch. That way you can learn about yourself and lose weight at the same time!

~ **Before bedtime writing.** At the end of a busy day, expressive writing can be a welcome escape. Many people fear that bedtime writing will give them nightmares. In fact, this does not happen with most people. If it does happen for you, however, then don't write just before bed. In one study of late night disclosure, researchers found that people actually went to sleep more quickly and slept better than people who were not given the opportunity to disclose their thoughts and feelings (Pennebaker 1997).

~ **Middle of the night writing.** I have spoken with a person who set his alarm clock to go off at 3:00 in the morning. He would silently get out of bed and write for twenty minutes. He swears by his technique. Try it if you want.

~ **Talking into a tape recorder in bed.** Go to bed with a tape recorder in your hand. Once the lights are out, simply talk about your thoughts and feelings into the microphone. This is recommended for people who do not have a sleeping partner.

It never hurts to exercise your mind and to break out of your usual routines. Experiment with new times and places to write. Judge for yourself what works best and why.

~ Chapter 10 ~

Writing Creatively: The Power of Fiction, Poetry, Dance, and Art

The expressive writing techniques presented in this workbook encourage you to express yourself in words. Through writing, you can begin to construct meaningful stories of your deeply personal experiences. Writing about your own upheavals, of course, is not the only way in which you can express yourself. Dancing, singing, painting, acting, and many other art forms can help you get a grip on your emotional upheavals.

In this chapter, you are encouraged to draw on your creative side. Allow your emotional experiences from your past to be expressed through other forms of writing or art. As you will see, in one way or another, each of these techniques relies on the power of words. However, our human brain's inventiveness can help us to make better and more insightful stories.

Fiction Writing: Constructing Imaginary Stories

The more you write about emotional and personal topics, the more you can appreciate the fine line between expressive writing and creative writing. One can't help but wonder where personal narrative ends and fiction begins. Would it be healthy to write fictionalized stories in the same way that it can be valuable to explore your own experiences? Possibly. A fascinating study conducted in the mid-1990s by Melanie Greenberg, Arthur Stone, and Camille Wortman (1996) and their colleagues had people write about traumas that had never happened to them. They were instructed to write about imaginary traumatic events as if they had really taken place in their own lives. Amazingly, people writing about these imaginary traumas exhibited significant health improvements.

Before discussing why writing imaginary stories might be good for your health, try the following twenty-minute writing exercise. In the box below, you will find the basic information about four different traumas. Your task is to choose one of the traumas, ideally one that is the *least* relevant to your life. Do not choose any trauma that has happened to you or a close friend.

Four Imaginary Traumatic Experiences

1. On returning home from work, you learn that the house you have owned for fifteen years has burned to the ground. All of your possessions, clothes, jewelry, pictures, and reminders of your past, have been destroyed. The police arrest you on charges of arson, even though you aren't guilty. Eventually, you are freed, but you have had to move in with a cousin while you think about what to do.

2. You go to a restaurant with three fun-loving friends. After eating, the others talk you into running out of the restaurant without paying. The four of you jump into your car and begin to drive away. The waitress runs out to flag you down. You accidentally hit her, which will put her into a wheelchair for the rest of her life. You get away and are never caught. You never see those friends again. You move to another town but the memory of the event continues to haunt you.

3. You have been married for seven years in what you think has been a good marriage. You accidentally discover that your spouse has been involved in a love affair with your best friend for more than a year. You learn that all of your friends and family have suspected this affair for the entire time. After you confront them, your best friend and your spouse abandon you. It is now two years after your divorce and you are about to go out on your first date.

4. When you were ten, your mother remarried. She is happier than you have ever seen her. One night after drinking heavily, your stepfather comes into your room and fondles you. He threatens that if you ever tell anyone, he will deny it. For the next five years, this happens a dozen more times. You never tell your mother. You think about this every day of your life and wonder how it is influencing you now.

WRITING INSTRUCTIONS. Choose one of the four scenarios described above that is the least relevant to your own life. Now imagine that this event happened to you. Really let go and try to feel the emotions you would experience and think the thoughts that you would currently be living with. Take at least ten minutes to relax deeply while thinking about this event. Create scenes in your mind and make them as vivid as you can. Finally, put yourself in the present and consider what it would be like for you now in trying to deal with this trauma.

For the next twenty minutes, write about this trauma as if it had really happened to you. Explore your deepest emotions and thoughts about this imaginary event. How might it be related to other events in your life? How did this trauma affect you when it happened? How does it affect you now? What meaning can you extract from this experience?

After thinking deeply about this experience, begin writing. Write continuously for a minimum of twenty minutes.

When you have finished your writing, analyze how it affected you. To what degree were you able to adopt this trauma as your own? Did you find it valuable or meaningful to write about it?

One reason that writing about imaginary traumas may be helpful is that we all have experienced terrible events that involved loss, humiliation, secrecy, betrayal, and rage, at one time or another. Even though you may not have had your house destroyed, you know what it is like to feel alone or falsely accused of something. Writing about imaginary traumas may help us give meaning to confusing emotional experiences in our own lives.

If you found this exercise valuable, try it again using one of the other traumas. Or, for that matter, pick a tragedy out of today's newspaper and write about it as if it happened to you. In addition to helping you come to terms with some of your own emotional issues, it should also make you more empathic about others' troubles.

Experimenting with Poetry

Although there has been very little scientific research on the healing power of poetry, it is commonly used in psychotherapy. You might understand intuitively that expressing emotions about powerful experiences through poetry should have positive health effects. Unlike straight prose writing, poetry can often capture the contradictions inherent in most emotions and experiences.

The majority of people who enjoy expressive writing also appreciate poetry. For this next exercise, recall or find a favorite poem. As you think about or read a meaningful poem, allow yourself to fall into the emotional state of the poem, and feel its cadence. If you don't have a poem handy, read and enjoy Robert Frost's well-known, "The Road Not Taken":

> Two roads diverged in a yellow wood,
> And sorry I could not travel both
> And be one traveler, long I stood
> And looked down one as far as I could
> To where it bent in the undergrowth;
>
> Then took the other, as just as fair,
> And having perhaps the better claim,
> Because it was grassy and wanted wear;
> Though as for that, the passing there
> Had worn them really about the same,
>
> And both that morning equally lay
> In leaves no step had trodden black.
> Oh, I kept the first for another day!

Yet knowing how way leads to way,
I doubted if I should ever come back.

I shall be telling this with a sigh
Somewhere ages and ages hence:
Two roads diverged in a wood, and I—
I took the one less traveled by,
And that has made all the difference.

WRITING INSTRUCTIONS. For this next writing assignment, transform a personal experience of yours into poetry. It doesn't have to rhyme. It can be as freeform as you want it to be. Turn off your mind's censor and touch an emotion, thought, or dream that is deep within you right now. Let the feelings crystallize into words. Let's dispense with the time limit. You may write for as long as you want.

Nonverbal Expressions and Words: Exploring Dance and Art

Are words necessary for healing to take place? If you could express your feelings about a trauma through dance, music, or art, would you get the same benefits as through writing? This question has been tested with a group of college students using a form of dance therapy. The results suggested that nonverbal expression is a powerful tool for making people feel better. However, when the students employed both bodily movement and writing, the healing effects were enhanced even further.

There is good reason to believe that translating emotional experiences into language can strengthen long-term cognitive changes more efficiently than nonverbal expression alone. In fact, most nonverbal therapies, art and dance therapy in particular, employ both nonverbal expression and language. Generally, the person is encouraged to first express an emotional upheaval through drawing or movement. When finished, the person is encouraged to talk about their artistic product. It may well be that the combination of nonverbal expression together with writing (or talking) may be one of the most powerful healing strategies available. Unfortunately, this thesis has not been adequately tested yet. In this section, two brief exercises are recommended, one involving dance and the other art. Try them out and see if they are worthwhile.

EXPRESSIVE MOVEMENT AND WRITING EXERCISE. For this exercise, it is important that you find a place where you can move around freely for at least ten minutes. It could be a living room with the furniture moved out of the way. It could be a space outside your home, or even an empty garage or classroom. Ideally, it will be a place where you can move around without others watching you (assuming you are at all self-conscious). If such a large person-free space isn't realistic, try using your shower. Note, too, that although this is referred to as a form of dance, no music is necessary.

For ten minutes, your task will be to express your deepest thoughts and feelings through movement about the issue or event that has the most significance in your life. You may use a traumatic experience, or one that was problematic or upsetting. It may be a current situation or conflict, or it can be from your past, but still very much on your mind. The important thing is to express in movement what you have never been able to say in words, so that now you will say it with the movements of your body. How you move and what you do is entirely up to you. There is no right or wrong way to express your feelings with movement. It's your body and only you know your experience and what it is that you feel within yourself.

Start with what makes sense to you. You can move in quick steps all over the floor, or stand still and undulate. You can use the room in any way you see fit. You may move quickly or slowly, strongly or softly. You might use parts of your body that you normally don't consciously use expressively, like your spine, your feet, your face, your shoulders. The only requirement is to *keep moving* the whole time; even if you are expressing a stuck, tired, or rigid feeling, there is always a way to translate it into movement.

After your ten minutes of movement, find a place to write for a minimum of another ten minutes. In your writing, explore your thoughts and feelings about the movement exercise you just completed. What was going on in your mind and body? What were you expressing? Did your body tell you something that you might not have been aware of? Use this time to try to understand both the emotional upheaval as well as your reaction to it. Once you begin writing, continue without stopping for at least ten minutes.

Many people find the expressive movement experience strangely powerful. You might find yourself trying to analyze what you did and why for some hours after you finish moving. Sometimes your movement may have great significance, other times it might not. If you find this form of expression useful, try doing it for several days in a row.

ARTISTIC EXPRESSION AND WRITING EXERCISE. Just as expressive movement can help to draw out issues you may not have considered, other forms of artistic expression can do the same. Drawing, painting, sculpting, and other visual arts have long been known to express peoples' deepest thoughts and emotions. Although I believe that artistic expression is physically beneficial, virtually no strong experimental studies have yet demonstrated it. Despite this, there are enough case studies for us to trust our instincts.

For the art-writing exercise, you should first spend some time drawing followed by a period of writing. You may or may not be able to draw a straight line, but that's not even relevant here. You can, however, express yourself through drawing or even doodling.

For the next ten minutes, your goal is use the blank space on the next page to express an emotionally important event, conflict, or feeling. Your drawing can be abstract, concrete, or seemingly random. The important thing is for you to really let go and express your deepest emotions and thoughts by drawing. Don't judge yourself during the time you are drawing; just let your pencil or pen do the work. Once you begin, keep drawing without stopping. Use additional paper if you need to. The important thing is that you really free yourself and draw.

At the end of the ten minutes, go back and study your drawing. What was going through your mind as you were working? What were you feeling? Think about this experience for some minutes. Now begin to use expressive writing. Translate your drawing experience into words. Draw on your emotions and thoughts. Address your issues about your emotional upheaval as well as writing about your experience of drawing.

This particular exercise relied on drawing. If you prefer, you may try other art forms. Many people like the sensuality of finger painting, the playfulness or dimensionality of clay, the vividness of acrylic or watercolors, or some other artistic medium. For the purpose of this exercise, the drawing period was only ten-minutes long. You might want to devote an entire afternoon to expressing yourself about an important emotional experience. Indeed, you need not limit yourself to traditional art forms. People often express their deepest thoughts and feelings through woodwork, gardening, cooking, sewing, or playing with sand. Whatever you chose to do, consider writing about it afterwards. Putting emotional experiences into words provides additional structure to an experience that can yield long-term benefits.

Resources

Expressive writing can be a valuable tool for helping people deal with traumas and emotional upheavals. However, although many people receive great benefit from writing, others don't. If, after trying expressive writing, you feel as though you haven't gained any benefits at all, or if you still need help in coping with your experience, please seek the professional advice of a physician, psychologist, or counselor.

Depression and Posttraumatic Stress Disorder (PTSD)

Traumas have the potential to set off a cascade of biological changes that result in a host of mental and physical problems. If you are deeply depressed or disoriented because of a traumatic experience, writing should not be your first course of action. In such a state, it is very difficult, if not impossible, to put the many pieces of your horrible experience together. It is also likely that your judgment of the experience may have been impaired.

Major Depression

In the days immediately following a shattering experience, most of us feel sad, upset, and really down in the dumps. However, if you have been extremely depressed for several weeks, and your experience of depression includes crying, overwhelming feelings of sadness or emptiness, and a striking loss of energy, you may be experiencing a major depressive disorder. Other symptoms can include a loss of interest in pleasure, loss of appetite, insomnia, inability to concentrate, and even recurrent thoughts about death. Many people with this disorder have trouble even getting out of bed in the morning.

If you feel as though you may be suffering from major depression, seek professional help. There are a number of promising treatments including medication. Indeed, there have been some impressive advances in drug treatment over the last fifty years. Medications can offer a relatively fast way to diminish the effects of some of the most devastating moods of a trauma. Once some of these symptoms have lifted, expressive writing and other treatments can be far more effective.

Posttraumatic Stress Disorder

Only since the 1980s have the medical and psychological communities begun to appreciate how life-threatening traumas can produce their own sets of problems. Posttraumatic stress disorder, or PTSD, occasionally surfaces in the days and weeks after an extreme trauma in which the person directly witnessed or experienced a life-threatening event. Car accidents, rape, robbery, and kidnapping frequently result in PTSD-related symptoms. In the weeks after the event, people with PTSD will often have vivid memories or dreams of the event. They report feeling extremely anxious much of the time, often accompanied by a sense of dread, which causes them to start avoiding any reminders of the trauma. Other symptoms often seen with depression may appear.

PTSD can be debilitating both emotionally and socially. As with major depression, PTSD is generally treatable in several ways. Both medication and psychotherapy are recommended. Once the most severe symptoms are in check, expressive writing may be particularly beneficial.

Where to Find Help

If you feel that you need help in some way, consider contacting any of the following people or agencies. Every moderately large city has a number of groups or centers that can help you.

Immediate, life-threatening help. If you are suicidal, feel as though you are a danger to yourself or others, or feel as though you are truly falling apart, call 911.

In crisis, need to talk to someone by phone. In most areas, there are telephone crisis counselors. These are generally indexed under names such as Crisis Hotline, Community Mental Health Services, sometimes Victim Services. If your distress is the result of a specific type of trauma, there is likely to be an organization with a toll-free number to call. Some current groups include the following:

Agency	Trauma specialty	Phone Number
American Red Cross	Natural disasters, fires, chemical spills, community-wide disasters	866-438-4636
Depression Hotline	Depression and depressive feelings	800-826-3632
National Domestic Violence Hotline	Spouse abuse, child abuse, other forms of family violence	800-799-7233
National Organization for Victim Assistance	Victims and witnesses of crimes	800-879-6682
Rape, Abuse, and Incest National Network	Sexual abuse	800-656-4673
Suicide Awareness: Voices of Education	Suicide crisis and education	800-784-2433

If you have access to a computer, there are literally dozens of crisis groups available to get more information. Many of these groups can provide you with someone to talk to about your problems. Use any search engine, and simply enter the type of crisis you are dealing with, for example, "cancer diagnosis," or "depression."

Need to see a physician or therapist. If you are experiencing a severe depression or symptoms of PTSD, see your physician or a psychiatrist, especially if you are open to taking medication. If you do not have a regular physician, consult the yellow pages or call your local physician referral network. If you would prefer to discuss your issues with someone, a psychologist or another licensed mental health specialist is recommended.

Additional Readings for a General Audience

There are a number of excellent books available that can supplement many of the ideas discussed in this workbook. Some that I particularly recommend include the following:

Abercrombie, B. 2002. *Writing Out the Storm: Reading and Writing Your Way Through Serious Illness or Injury.* New York: St. Martin's Press.

Adams, K. 1994. *Mightier Than the Sword.* New York: Warner Books.

Cameron, J. 2002. *The Artist's Way: A Spiritual Path to Higher Creativity.* New York: Jeremy P. Tarcher.

Capacchione, L. 1988. *The Power of Your Other Hand.* North Hollywood, CA: Newcastle Publishing.

Csikszentmihalyi, M. 1997. *Finding Flow: The Psychology of Engagement with Everyday Life.* New York: Basic Books.

Dayton, T. 2002. *Daily Affirmations for Forgiving and Moving On.* Deerfield Beach, FL: Health Communications.

DeSalvo, L. 2000. *Writing as a Way of Healing: How Telling Our Stories Transforms Our Lives.* Boston: Beacon Press.

Dreher, H. 1995. *The Immune Power Personality.* New York: Penguin Books.

Fox, J. 1997. *Poetic Medicine: The Healing Art of Poem-Making.* New York: Jeremy P. Tarcher.

Goldberg, N. 1986. *Writing Down the Bones: Freeing the Writer Within.* Boston, MA: Shambhala Publications.

Goleman, D. 1995. *Emotional Intelligence.* New York: Bantam.

Myers, L. J. 2003. *Becoming Whole: Writing Your Healing Story.* San Diego: Healing Threads.

Pennebaker, J. W. 1997. *Opening Up: The Healing Power of Expressing Emotions.* New York: Guilford.

Rosenthal, N. R. 2002. *The Emotional Revolution: How the New Science of Feeling Can Transform Your Life.* New York: Citadel Press.

Sapolsky, R. M. 1998. *Why Zebras Don't Get Ulcers* (revised edition). New York: Freeman.

Seligman, M. E. P. 2002. *Authentic Happiness: Using the New Positive Psychology to Realize Your Potential for Lasting Fulfillment.* New York: Free Press.

Zimmerman, S. 2002. *Writing to Heal the Soul: Transforming Grief and Loss Through Writing.* Pittsburgh, PA: Three Rivers Press.

References

The expressive writing research has been based on hundreds of studies. The articles listed below were either cited in the book or are directly relevant to the expressive writing literature. To get a more comprehensive list of related research, go to my web page: www.psy.utexas.edu/Pennebaker.

Brewin, C. R., and H. Lennard. 1999. Effects of mode of writing on emotional narratives. *Journal of Traumatic Stress* 12: 355-361.

Cameron, L. D., and G. Nicholls. 1998. Expression of stressful experiences through writing: Effects of a self-regulation manipulation for pessimists and optimists. *Health Psychology* 17: 84-92.

Campbell, R. S., and J. W. Pennebaker. 2003. The secret life of pronouns: Flexibility in writing style and physical health. *Psychological Science* 14: 60-65.

Christensen A. J., D. L. Edwards, J. S. Wiebe, E. G. Benotsch, L. McKelvey, M. Andrews, and D. M. Lubaroff. 1996. Effect of verbal self-disclosure on natural killer cell activity: Moderating influence of cynical hostility. *Psychosomatic Medicine* 58: 150-155.

Cole, S. W., M. E. Kemeny, S. E.Taylor, and B. R. Visscher. 1996. Accelerated course of human immunodeficiency virus infection in gay men who conceal their homosexual identity. *Psychosomatic Medicine* 58: 219-231.

Crow, D. M. 2000. *Physiological and Health Effects of Writing about Stress.* Unpublished doctoral dissertation. Dallas, TX: Southern Methodist University.

De Moor, C., J. Sterner, M. Hall, C. Warneke, Z. Gilani, R. Amato, and L. Cohen. 2002. A pilot study of the effects of expressive writing in a phase II trial of vaccine therapy for metastatic renal cell carcinoma. *Health Psychology* 21: 615-619.

Esterling, B. A., M. H. Antoni, M. A. Fletcher, S. Margulies, and N. Schneiderman. 1994. Emotional disclosure through writing or speaking modulates latent Epstein-Barr virus antibody titers. *Journal of Consulting and Clinical Psychology* 62: 130-140.

Foa, E. B., and M. J. Kozak. 1986. Emotional processing of fear: Exposure to corrective information. *Psychological Bulletin* 99: 20-35.

Francis, M. E., and J. W. Pennebaker. 1992. Putting stress into words: Writing about personal upheavals and health. *American Journal of Health Promotion* 6: 280-287.

Gidron, Y., T. Peri, J. F. Connolly, and A. Y. Shalev. 1996. Written disclosure in posttraumatic stress disorder: Is it beneficial for the patient? *Journal of Nervous and Mental Disease* 184: 505- 507.

Greenberg, M. A., A. A. Stone, and C. B. Wortman. 1996. Health and psychological effects of emotional disclosure: A test of the inhibition-confrontation approach. *Journal of Personality and Social Psychology* 71: 588-602.

King, L. A., and K. N. Miner. 2000. Writing about the perceived benefits of traumatic events: Implications for physical health. *Personality and Social Psychology Bulletin* 26: 220-230.

Klein, K., and A. Boals. 2001. Expressive writing can increase working memory capacity. *Journal of Experimental Psychology: General* 130: 520-533.

Lepore, S. J. 1997. Expressive writing moderates the relation between intrusive thoughts and depressive symptoms. *Journal of Personality and Social Psychology* 73: 1030-1037.

Lepore, S. J., and J. M. Smyth, Eds. 2002. *The Writing Cure: How Expressive Writing Promotes Health and Emotional Well-Being.* Washington, DC: American Psychological Association.

Lumley, M. A., and K. M. Provenzano. 2003. Stress management through emotional disclosure improves academic performance among college students with physical symptoms. *Journal of Educational Psychology* 95: 641–649.

McAdams, D. P. 1993. *The Stories We Live By: Personal Myths and the Making of the Self.* New York: Morrow.

Newman, M. L., J. W. Pennebaker, D. S. Berry, and J. M. Richards. 2003. Lying words: Predicting deception from linguistic styles. *Personality and Social Psychology Bulletin* 29: 665-675.

North, A. C., D. J. Hargreaves, and J. McKendrick. 1997. In store music affects product choice. *Nature* 390: 132.

Pennebaker, J. W. 1997. *Opening Up: The Healing Power of Expressing Emotions,* revised edition. New York: Guilford Press.

Pennebaker, J. W., and A. Graybeal. 2001. Patterns of natural language use: Disclosure, personality, and social integration. *Current Directions in Psychological Science* 10: 90-93.

Pennebaker, J. W., and S. K. Beall. 1986. Confronting a traumatic event: Toward an understanding of inhibition and disease. *Journal of Abnormal Psychology* 95: 274-281.

Pennebaker, J. W., and J. R. Susman. 1988. Disclosure of traumas and psychosomatic processes. *Social Science and Medicine* 26: 327-332.

Pennebaker, J. W., M. Colder, and L. K. Sharp. 1990. Accelerating the coping process. *Journal of Personality and Social Psychology* 58: 528-537.

Pennebaker, J. W., C. F. Hughes, and R. C. O'Heeron. 1987. The psychophysiology of confession: Linking inhibitory and psychosomatic processes. *Journal of Personality and Social Psychology* 52: 781-793.

Pennebaker, J. W., J. K. Kiecolt-Glaser, and R. Glaser. 1988. Confronting traumatic experience and immunocompetence: A reply to Neale, Cox, Valdimarsdottir, and Stone. *Journal of Consulting and Clinical Psychology* 45: 638-639.

Pennebaker, J. W., T. J. Mayne, .and M. E. Francis. 1997. Linguistic predictors of adaptive bereavement. *Journal of Personality and Social Psychology* 72: 863-871.

Petrie, K. J., R. J. Booth, J. W. Pennebaker, K. P. Davison, and M. Thomas. 1995. Disclosure of trauma and immune response to Hepatitis B vaccination program. *Journal of Consulting and Clinical Psychology* 63: 787-792.

Petrie, K. J., R. J. Booth, and J. W. Pennebaker. 1998. The immunological effects of thought suppression. *Journal of Personality and Social Psychology* 75: 1264-1272.

Petrie, K. J., I. Fontanilla, M. Thomas, R. J. Booth, and J. W. Pennebaker. In press. Effect of written emotional expression on immune functioning in patients with HIV infection. *Psychosomatic Medicine*.

Richards, J. M., W. E. Beal, J. Seagal, and J. W. Pennebaker. 2000. The effects of disclosure of traumatic events on illness behavior among psychiatric prison inmates. *Journal of Abnormal Psychology* 109: 156-160.

Smyth, J. M. 1998. Written emotional expression: Effect sizes, outcome types, and moderating variables. *Journal of Consulting and Clinical Psychology* 66: 174-184.

Smyth, J. M., A. A. Stone, A. Hurewitz, and A. Kaell. 1999. Effects of writing about stressful experiences on symptom reduction in patients with asthma or rheumatoid arthritis: A randomized trial. *JAMA: Journal of the American Medical Association* 281: 1304-1309.

Spera, S. P., E. D. Buhrfeind, and J. W. Pennebaker. 1994. Expressive writing and coping with job loss. *Academy of Management Journal* 37: 722-733.

Stanton, A. L., S. Danoff-Burg, L. A. Sworowski, C. A. Collins, A. D. Branstetter, A. Rodriguez-Hanley, S. B. Kirk, and J. L. Austenfeld. 2002. Randomized, controlled trial of written emotional expression and benefit finding in breast cancer patients. *Journal of Clinical Oncology* 20: 4160-4168.

Stroebe, M., W. Stroebe, E. Zech, and H. Schut. 2002. Does disclosure of emotions facilitate recovery from bereavement? Evidence from two prospective studies. *Journal of Consulting and Clinical Psychology* 70: 169-178.

Wegner, D. M. 2002. The illusion of conscious will. Cambridge, MA: MIT Press.

Wicklund, R. A. 1979. The influence of self-awareness on human behavior. *American Scientist* 6: 187-193.

Wortman, C. B., and R. C. Silver. 1989. The myths of coping with loss. *Journal of Consulting and Clinical Psychology* 57: 349-357.

James W. Pennebaker, Ph.D., is professor of psychology at the University of Texas at Austin. His research has earned honors from the American Psychological Association and the Pavlovian Society. He is the recipient of multiple teaching awards from the University of Texas and is the author of more than 150 professional publications. His work has earned research grants from the National Science Foundation and the National Institute of Mental Health.

Some Other
New Harbinger Titles

Freeing the Angry Mind, Item 4380 $14.95

Living Beyond Your Pain, Item 4097 $19.95

Transforming Anxiety, Item 4445 $12.95

Integrative Treatment for Borderline Personality Disorder, Item 4461 $24.95

Depressed and Anxious, Item 3635 $19.95

Is He Depressed or What?, Item 4240 $15.95

Cognitive Therapy for Obsessive-Compulsive Disorder, Item 4291 $39.95

Child and Adolescent Psychopharmacology Made Simple, Item 4356 $14.95

ACT* on Life Not on Anger, Item 4402 $14.95

Overcoming Medical Phobias, Item 3872 $14.95

Acceptance & Commitment Therapy for Anxiety Disorders, Item 4275 $58.95

The OCD Workbook, Item 4224 $19.95

Neural Path Therapy, Item 4267 $14.95

Overcoming Obsessive Thoughts, Item 3813 $14.95

The Interpersonal Solution to Depression, Item 4186 $19.95

Get Out of Your Mind & Into Your Life, Item 4259 $19.95

Dialectical Behavior Therapy in Private Practice, Item 4208 $54.95

The Anxiety & Phobia Workbook, 4th edition, Item 4135 $19.95

Loving Someone with OCD, Item 3295 $15.95

Overcoming Animal & Insect Phobias, Item 3880 $12.95

Overcoming Compulsive Washing, Item 4054 $14.95

Angry All the Time, Item 3929 $13.95

Handbook of Clinical Psychopharmacology for Therapists, 4th edition, Item 3996 $55.95

Writing For Emotional Balance, Item 3821 $14.95

Surviving Your Borderline Parent, Item 3287 $14.95

When Anger Hurts, 2nd edition, Item 3449 $16.95

Calming Your Anxious Mind, Item 3384 $12.95

Ending the Depression Cycle, Item 3333 $17.95

Your Surviving Spirit, Item 3570 $18.95

Coping with Anxiety, Item 3201 $10.95

The Agoraphobia Workbook, Item 3236 $19.95

Call **toll free, 1-800-748-6273,** or log on to our online bookstore at **www.newharbinger.com** to order. Have your Visa or Mastercard number ready. Or send a check for the titles you want to New Harbinger Publications, Inc., 5674 Shattuck Ave., Oakland, CA 94609. Include $4.50 for the first book and 75¢ for each additional book, to cover shipping and handling. (California residents please include appropriate sales tax.) Allow two to five weeks for delivery.

Prices subject to change without notice.

Printed in the United States
137003LV00001BA/41/A